THE PERFECT CHILDREN'S DOG

By Jan Mahood

Quarterly

How do you pick the right dog for your family? Choosing the right breed, size and temperament for your children is extremely important in order to enjoy a happy and satisfying relationship with your dog. *The Perfect Children's Dog Quarterly* is designed to help you make an informed and educated choice about what type of dog you should bring into your particular home environment. It covers everything you'll need to know, including how to research the breed that is best for your family, a list of popular family-friendly breeds and their personalities, choosing the right breeder, all about adoption and rescue agencies, and what do once you bring your new dog home, especially the events and activities your dog and child can participate in together. With *The Perfect Children's Dog,* you can prepare to take the first steps toward a long and loving relationship with your family's ideal canine companion.

What are Quarterlies?

Books, the usual way information of this sort is transmitted, can be too slow. Sometimes by the time a book is written and published, the material contained therein is a year or two old...and no new material has been added during that time. Only a book in a magazine form can bring breaking stories and current information. A magazine is streamlined in production, so we have adopted certain magazine publishing techniques in the creation of this Dog Quarterly. Magazines also can be much cheaper than books because they are supported by advertising. To combine these assets into a great publication, we issued this Quarterly in both magazine and book format at different prices.

Distributed in the UNITED STATES to the Pet Trade by T.F.H. Publications, Inc., One T.F.H. Plaza, Neptune City, NJ 07753; distributed in the UNITED STATES to the Bookstore and Library Trade by National Book Network, Inc. 4720 Boston Way, Lanham MD 20706; in CANADA to the Pet Trade by H & L Pet Supplies Inc., 27 Kingston Crescent, Kitchener, Ontario N2B 2T6; Rolf C. Hagen Inc., 3225 Sartelon St. Laurent-Montreal Quebec H4R 1E8; in CANADA to the Book Trade by Vanwell Publishing Ltd., 1 Northrup Crescent, St. Catharines, Ontario L2M 6P5 ; in ENGLAND by T.F.H. Publications, PO Box 15, Waterlooville PO7 6BQ; in AUSTRALIA AND THE SOUTH PACIFIC by T.F.H. (Australia), Pty. Ltd., Box 149, Brookvale 2100 N.S.W., Australia; in NEW ZEALAND by Brooklands Aquarium Ltd. 5 McGiven Drive, New Plymouth, RD1 New Zealand; in Japan by T.F.H. Publications, Japan—Jiro Tsuda, 10-12-3 Ohjidai, Sakura, Chiba 285, Japan; in SOUTH AFRICA by Lopis (Pty) Ltd., P.O. Box 39127, Booysens, 2016, Johannesburg, South Africa. Published by T.F.H. Publications, Inc.

MANUFACTURED IN THE
UNITED STATES OF AMERICA
BY T.F.H. PUBLICATIONS, INC.

yearBOOKS,INC.
Dr. Herbert R. Axelrod,
Founder & Chairman

Neal Pronek
Chief Editor

Stacy Kennedy
Editor

yearBOOKS are all photo composed, color separated and designed on Scitex equipment in Neptune, N.J. with the following staff:

DIGITAL PRE-PRESS
Patricia Northrup
Supervisor

Robert Onyrscuk
Jose Reyes

COMPUTER ART
Patti Escabi
Sandra Taylor Gale
Candida Moreira
Joanne Muzyka
Francine Shulman

ADVERTISING SALES
George Campbell
National Advertising Manager
Amy Manning
Advertising Director
Sandy Cutillo
Advertising Coordinator
Nancy Rivadeneira
*Periodicals Advertising
Sales Manager*
Cheryl Blyth
*Periodicals Sales
Representative*

©yearBOOKS, Inc.
1 TFH Plaza
Neptune, N.J. 07753
Completely manufactured in
Neptune, N.J.
USA

Cover design by Sherise Buhagiar

Lori Ann Trezona with her Golden Retriever friend.

CONTENTS

THE PERFECT FAMILY DOG

This book is designed to help you choose a dog: to give you advice on where to find healthy, well-socialized dogs who are ready to join your family; how to prepare your kids and your house for the new arrrival; and how to have and be a teammate and companion for life.

WHEN THE DOG IS THERE FIRST

A Wire Fox Terrier named Spike was there first. Before I came along, he had his place, which was pretty much in the center of the family circle. People told my parents, "You'd better get rid of that dog before the baby comes. He'll be jealous and might bite the new arrival. He's too rough for a baby." To my parents' credit, they didn't listen. Spike stayed.

If they had chosen the ideal child for a dog, it would not have been a baby—noisy when the dog wants a nap, hungry when the dog wants to be fed, prone to making sudden unexpected moves and sounds, and allowed to do things the dog isn't allowed to do—mess in the house, enjoy a meal in the middle of the night, sleep in the parents' room, ride in a carriage, and be fussed over by grandparents.

And if they had researched what kind of dog they should get for a baby, they wouldn't have gotten a dog at all until I was older. They probably would not have gotten a terrier, because terriers tend to be scrappy, busy, determined dogs that can be a challenge to train. Also, proper terrier coat grooming takes time—a commodity that is in short supply when there's a human baby in the house.

So Spike didn't always look ready for the show ring. But he slept by my crib. He watched as I learned to crawl. And when I was ready to walk, I grabbed his wiry coat and pulled myself to my feet while he stood by patiently.

Spike accepted the new baby because my parents didn't make a major production of my arrival. They treated Spike just as they always had, and introduced us in a matter-of-fact way, watching him to make sure he didn't get overexcited, and watching me to make sure I

Author Jan Mahood at three years of age with her first dog, Spike.

Tara and Hayley Wilson with their Siberian Husky, Hunter.

years, until the children are old enough to participate in the dog's training and care. Even then, a dog that is ideal for older or bigger kids might not be the right choice for your seven- or eight-year-old.

Before you even think of selecting the perfect dog for your kids, ask yourself if you have the perfect kids for a dog. Keep their ages, personalities and energy levels in mind. Does a dog fit your family's lifestyle?

Ask yourself if everyone in the family really wants a dog. Can you afford to keep a dog? Do you and the kids have time to train, groom and exercise a dog?

A dog will be your kids' best friend for a lifetime — and it's your job to impress upon them what this means in terms of responsibility. When in doubt, don't—at least for now. When you're ready, there will still be millions of dogs looking for kids to love.

didn't pull his hair or poke him in the eye. He knew I was special. He also knew I was not there to replace him in my parents' affections.

Spike and I became inseparable. As I got older, I walked and fed him. I learned never to tease or corner him. I taught him to sit and stay. He taught me to be kind. We respected each other.

Spike lived to be 15. I can still smell his comfortable doggy smell, feel his wiry hair against my face as I circled my arms round him. Spike made an impression. As long as I live, I will always have dogs in my life.

WHEN IN DOUBT, WAIT

A retired show dog, Spike was already a beloved family pet when I came along. As far as my parents were concerned, it would have been out of the question to place him in another home.

However, for most families,

a baby is not the ideal companion for a dog. To minimize frazzled nerves and the potential for injury to child and dog alike, most parents prefer to wait a few

Make sure the decision to add a dog to your household is one the whole family agrees upon. Golden Retrievers with friends.

THE FIRST DOG: DOING IT RIGHT

Your child wants a dog, and the stuffed variety from F.A.O. Schwarz will no longer do. It's time, first of all, to impress upon your child that this want is different from all the other wants he or she has ever experienced. This is not a bike to be garaged or left out in the rain. It is not a teddy bear left in a corner. It is not a video game, swing set, or string of beads to be discarded, traded or given away once its novelty fades.

This time, if your child is to get what he wants, you must be absolutely convinced that

Your children should be ready, willing and able to share in the responsibilities of dog ownership. A Rottweiler puppy with a friend.

Parents should carefully consider what kind of dog will best fit their child's personality. This family includes their English Springer Spaniels in everything they do.

he is ready to share responsibility, for this time he wants a living, breathing creature that will give what it receives — on one hand, love, loyalty and companionship; on the other hand, disappointment, rejection and pain all around.

THE RIGHT CHILD FOR YOUR DOG

As a parent, your responsibility is, first of all, to make sure that you have the right child for your dog, whoever the dog may eventually be. What is your relationship with your child like? Does he or she

Pet ownership should be a family affair—every member should take part in the care of their pets. The Gross family with their cat and Labrador Retriever.

participate enthusiastically in family activities? Willingly accept instruction and correction from you? Demonstrate kindness and consideration toward other family members, friends and animals? Are you, your child, or another family member going through a "difficult phase," during which it would be unwise to add a four-legged friend to the unsettled mix? If this is the case, wait until the time is right to think about getting a dog. Don't expect a dog to make everything right in an unstable family situation. It happens only in the movies.

If your child shows that he or she is ready to share the responsibility of dog ownership and you have the time and patience to be teacher and trainer to both child and dog, take the next giant step. It's time to embark on a delightful adventure of learning and bonding, as family members work together toward the goal of choosing the perfect dog.

DOG SHOWS AND NEW FRIENDS

Abigail and Jeremiah Banegas were five and eight years old, respectively, "a good minimum age for a dog," their parents, Annie and Hector, decided. "We thought they were old enough to learn to be responsible and to interact without being a nuisance to the dog," said Annie.

When they set out to find that perfect dog, Hector and Annie thought the Westminster Kennel Club Show, a short train ride from their suburban New Jersey home, would be an ideal place to start. Every February at Manhattan's Madison Square Garden, the second-oldest U.S. sporting event (next to the Kentucky Derby) spotlights 2,500

representatives of the 140 breeds recognized by the American Kennel Club. Some of the finest dogs in the world can be seen at Westminster, and the Banegases looked forward to learning a lot during the two-day show.

Westminster, one of the few benched shows in the U.S., gives the public an opportunity to meet dogs, owners, breeders and handlers "behind the scenes." At most shows, dogs strut their stuff in the ring and then are whisked away to their crates or exercise pens. At benched shows, the dogs, attended by handlers or owners, stay backstage on benches before and after they go into the ring, while spectators stop by for a closer view of breeds that interest them.

Adjacent to the benching area is the AKC booth, where knowledgable representatives from the American Kennel

Jeremiah Banegas teaches Jimmy the Beagle to sit.

FAMILY-FRIENDLY BREEDS

Dogs and kids go together. All breeds can be devoted companions if selected from proven bloodlines, purchased from responsible breeders, raised from puppyhood with kids and given love, respect and proper obedience training.

Having said that, I urge you to think twice and then again when selecting a breed. Some working and herding breeds reach their full potential only with experienced dog owners and trainers. They take their jobs very seriously, and behavior that comes naturally to them may clash with your family's routine. For example, a Herding breed might snap and nip at a small child's heels as he tries to herd the tot. A Working dog who considers herself a protective nanny to your children might take a swipe at you if you try to discipline them. Even the most docile large breed may be just to big for a youngster to control. And Toy breeds aren't really toys, even though it's easy for a child to treat them as such. Only gentle, thoughtful children are appropriate owners for these tiny companion dogs. Cost is a consideration, too. Expenses for food, grooming, boarding and veterinary care increase in direct proportion to size.

Breeds are organized according to group. Each group was originally bred for a specific purpose, and breeds

Most dogs, when raised with children and properly socialized, will be excellent companions. These two will be friends for life!

Pet ownership should be a family affair—every member should take part in the care of their pets. The Gross family with their cat and Labrador Retriever.

participate enthusiastically in family activities? Willingly accept instruction and correction from you? Demonstrate kindness and consideration toward other family members, friends and animals? Are you, your child, or another family member going through a "difficult phase," during which it would be unwise to add a four-legged friend to the unsettled mix? If this is the case, wait until the time is right to think about getting a dog. Don't expect a dog to make everything right in an unstable family situation. It happens only in the movies.

If your child shows that he or she is ready to share the responsibility of dog ownership and you have the time and patience to be teacher and trainer to both child and dog, take the next giant step. It's time to embark on a delightful adventure of learning and bonding, as

family members work together toward the goal of choosing the perfect dog.

DOG SHOWS AND NEW FRIENDS

Abigail and Jeremiah Banegas were five and eight years old, respectively, "a good minimum age for a dog," their parents, Annie and Hector, decided. "We thought they were old enough to learn to be responsible and to interact without being a nuisance to the dog," said Annie.

When they set out to find that perfect dog, Hector and Annie thought the Westminster Kennel Club Show, a short train ride from their suburban New Jersey home, would be an ideal place to start. Every February at Manhattan's Madison Square Garden, the second-oldest U.S. sporting event (next to the Kentucky Derby) spotlights 2,500

representatives of the 140 breeds recognized by the American Kennel Club. Some of the finest dogs in the world can be seen at Westminster, and the Banegases looked forward to learning a lot during the two-day show.

Westminster, one of the few benched shows in the U.S., gives the public an opportunity to meet dogs, owners, breeders and handlers "behind the scenes." At most shows, dogs strut their stuff in the ring and then are whisked away to their crates or exercise pens. At benched shows, the dogs, attended by handlers or owners, stay backstage on benches before and after they go into the ring, while spectators stop by for a closer view of breeds that interest them.

Adjacent to the benching area is the AKC booth, where knowledgable representatives from the American Kennel

Jeremiah Banegas teaches Jimmy the Beagle to sit.

Club (AKC) are on hand to answer questions about dogs and dog shows, run breed videos and distribute literature about choosing and caring for purebred dogs. Pet food companies set up displays where show spectators can learn about proper nutrition for all stages of a dog's life. All along the perimeter of the benching area are booths brimming with dog books, magazines, toys, treats, jewelry and breed-related clothing for both dogs and their humans.

WHEN THE TIME IS RIGHT

Annie and Hector had been discussing the relative merits of various breeds ever since they moved from New York City to the suburbs. They were looking at purebred dogs, because they knew each breed has certain traits. By matching breed

Kids and dogs will both benefit from regular exercise. Abby Banegas and her Beagle Jimmy take a walk around the block.

characteristics to their requirements in a family dog, they hoped to narrow their choice to a few breeds.

First, they discussed the qualities they wanted in a dog. Then they found out what breeds had those qualities. Next, they planned to look at dogs and talk to breeders. By following these steps, they reasoned, they'd leave as little as possible to chance in their final choice.

Hector had had German Shepherds when he was a

Different breeds have different needs. A breed like the Australian Shepherd needs plenty of exercise and activity to keep happy.

and feeds the dog and takes it to the veterinarians.

The Banegases discussed Toy breeds. Abby had enjoyed walking a friend's Min Pin, and both children loved the little dog's spunky attitude and enthusiasm for playing with them and their friends.

"Too small," insisted Hector, still thinking German Shepherd. "It's a hardy little dog, but its slender legs could be injured if one of the kids' friends gets too rough."

The search turned to

boy, and favored that breed. He knew that well-bred GSDs can be good family members —intelligent and trainable, loyal and protective in guarding home and family. Annie, who tips the scale at 100 lb. or so, preferred a smaller dog. She knew that, no matter the protestations of other family members, it is usually the mother who walks

medium-sized dogs. The Banegases were now leaning toward scenthounds. They liked their sporty looks, low-maintenance coats, and good-natured attitude. So off they went to Westminster, where they scheduled their day to watch exhibits of the breeds they liked best in the Hound group—the Harrier, English Foxhound, American

A reputable breeder will be able to give you all the information you require on the breed of dog in which you are interested. Jacob Miller with a litter of Norfolk Terriers.

Foxhound, Basset and Beagle. It was a tough choice, because they found qualities they liked in all these breeds.

After watching the dogs in the ring, they looked at the Beagles on the benches and talked with breeders. They arranged to meet one at his kennels, where they met a puppy named Jimmy. Beagles come in two sizes—13 inches and 15 inches. Jimmy was a sturdy little 13-inch guy, with a personality and size that fit their needs. He was small enough for Annie and the children to handle, and tough enough to withstand rough-and-tumble play. He'd get the exercise he needed by accompanying Hector on his daily runs and joining the whole family in their frequent outdoor activities. He cocked his head at them, waved his white-tipped tail, and even

seemed to smile! The decision was all but made.

The Banagases saw Jimmy's mother and father, so they had some idea what the pup would look like as an adult. They watched him interact with other dogs and with people, and saw that he was not the most dominant puppy in the group, but not at all timid, either. He was just as easy-going and cheerful as

Pick a breed that best suits your family's lifestyle, environment and level of activity. Abby and Jimmy are a perfect fit!

they had remembered. The breeder answered questions and volunteered information about the history, care and feeding of the Beagle.

After another visit with the breeder-exhibitor, a contract was drawn up and Annie, Hector, Jeremiah and Abby took home Jimmy the Beagle. They agreed to be co-owners

with the breeder, who wanted to show Jimmy. The routine goes like this: The breeder picks Jimmy up at the Banegases' home, takes him to shows and drops him off afterward. He's a show dog and family pet all in one jolly package!

BE READY FOR ANYTHING!

The Banegases knew that Beagles' inbred instinct is to track small game such as rabbits. Once they catch an interesting scent, the chase is on! "Their ears turn off when their noses turn on!" is an oft-repeated saying of Beagle owners.

Keeping in mind that a Beagle's middle name is Houdini, the Banegases made their house and yard escape-

FAMILY-FRIENDLY BREEDS

Dogs and kids go together. All breeds can be devoted companions if selected from proven bloodlines, purchased from responsible breeders, raised from puppyhood with kids and given love, respect and proper obedience training.

Having said that, I urge you to think twice and then again when selecting a breed. Some working and herding breeds reach their full potential only with experienced dog owners and trainers. They take their jobs very seriously, and behavior that comes naturally to them may clash with your family's routine. For example, a Herding breed might snap and nip at a small child's heels as he tries to herd the tot. A Working dog who considers herself a protective nanny to your children might take a swipe at you if you try to discipline them. Even the most docile large breed may be just to big for a youngster to control. And Toy breeds aren't really toys, even though it's easy for a child to treat them as such. Only gentle, thoughtful children are appropriate owners for these tiny companion dogs. Cost is a consideration, too. Expenses for food, grooming, boarding and veterinary care increase in direct proportion to size.

Breeds are organized according to group. Each group was originally bred for a specific purpose, and breeds

Most dogs, when raised with children and properly socialized, will be excellent companions. These two will be friends for life!

A reputable breeder will be able to give you all the information you require on the breed of dog in which you are interested. Jacob Miller with a litter of Norfolk Terriers.

Foxhound, Basset and Beagle. It was a tough choice, because they found qualities they liked in all these breeds.

After watching the dogs in the ring, they looked at the Beagles on the benches and talked with breeders. They arranged to meet one at his kennels, where they met a puppy named Jimmy. Beagles come in two sizes—13 inches and 15 inches. Jimmy was a sturdy little 13-inch guy, with a personality and size that fit their needs. He was small enough for Annie and the children to handle, and tough enough to withstand rough-and-tumble play. He'd get the exercise he needed by accompanying Hector on his daily runs and joining the whole family in their frequent outdoor activities. He cocked his head at them, waved his white-tipped tail, and even

seemed to smile! The decision was all but made.

The Banagases saw Jimmy's mother and father, so they had some idea what the pup would look like as an adult. They watched him interact with other dogs and with people, and saw that he was not the most dominant puppy in the group, but not at all timid, either. He was just as easy-going and cheerful as

Pick a breed that best suits your family's lifestyle, environment and level of activity. Abby and Jimmy are a perfect fit!

they had remembered. The breeder answered questions and volunteered information about the history, care and feeding of the Beagle.

After another visit with the breeder-exhibitor, a contract was drawn up and Annie, Hector, Jeremiah and Abby took home Jimmy the Beagle. They agreed to be co-owners

with the breeder, who wanted to show Jimmy. The routine goes like this: The breeder picks Jimmy up at the Banegases' home, takes him to shows and drops him off afterward. He's a show dog and family pet all in one jolly package!

BE READY FOR ANYTHING!

The Banegases knew that Beagles' inbred instinct is to track small game such as rabbits. Once they catch an interesting scent, the chase is on! "Their ears turn off when their noses turn on!" is an oft-repeated saying of Beagle owners.

Keeping in mind that a Beagle's middle name is Houdini, the Banegases made their house and yard escape-proof before they brought Jimmy home. They made sure there were no gaps under the fence that enclosed their backyard. The children were told to watch for their pup every time they opened the gate or the front door, so he wouldn't run out. When it was time for walkies, They made sure to clip on his leash and grip it firmly before opening the door.

One night, Hector and Jimmy went for a run. Hector bent to adjust his shoelaces, and the hard plastic grip of Jimmy's retractable leash slipped from his hand.

Jimmy was off! The plastic handle bumped and clattered along behind him, frightening him and making him run all the faster. Frantically calling Jimmy's name, Hector sprinted after the errant hound. To his

horror, he saw a car backing out of a driveway directly in their path. "Jimmy!" he shouted. His nose to the ground, the little Beagle ran under the car—and right out the other side!

Finally, he stopped at a mailbox and somehow tangled his leash around the bottom. Hector caught up. Sweating and panting, he bagged his Beagle, who was as glad to see his owner as Hector was glad to pick him up and hug him, resolving never again to relax his Beagle-awareness, even for a split-second.

Jimmy settled happily into the family. He gets proper nutrition, plenty of exercise, a basketful of dog toys, lots of love and a Beagle-size Queen Anne sofa all his own.

Annie's and Hector's methodical deliberation not

only ensured a good choice for Abby and Jeremiah, but also taught the kids an important lesson about how to make major decisions.

The Banegases did it right. They did their homework ahead of time. Along the way, they saw several dogs that appealed to them, but they never gave in to an impulse to take one home then and there. They talked to knowledgable owners, breeders and handlers. Along the way, they gained new friends. They selected the breed—and the dog—that was perfect for the kids—and the parents, too. So perfect, in fact, that they're now talking about getting a second Beagle.

Be forewarned: When you fall in love with a breed, you may experience the potato chip phenomenon—you can't have just one!

If you do your homework, selecting the right breed for you will be a snap! This Golden gives her friend a big hug.

Kids love hot dogs—especially the canine kind! A Dachshund gets a hug from his special friend.

FAMILY-FRIENDLY BREEDS

Dogs and kids go together. All breeds can be devoted companions if selected from proven bloodlines, purchased from responsible breeders, raised from puppyhood with kids and given love, respect and proper obedience training.

Having said that, I urge you to think twice and then again when selecting a breed. Some working and herding breeds reach their full potential only with experienced dog owners and trainers. They take their jobs very seriously, and behavior that comes naturally to them may clash with your family's routine. For example, a Herding breed might snap and nip at a small child's heels as he tries to herd the tot. A Working dog who considers herself a protective nanny to your children might take a swipe at you if you try to discipline them. Even the most docile large breed may be just to big for a youngster to control. And Toy breeds aren't really toys, even though it's easy for a child to treat them as such. Only gentle, thoughtful children are appropriate owners for these tiny companion dogs. Cost is a consideration, too. Expenses for food, grooming, boarding and veterinary care increase in direct proportion to size.

Breeds are organized according to group. Each group was originally bred for a specific purpose, and breeds

Most dogs, when raised with children and properly socialized, will be excellent companions. These two will be friends for life!

in that group have similar characteristics. The group names are self-explanatory: Sporting, Hound, Working, Terrier (It helps if you know a little Latin. Terrier comes from *terra* , Latin for earth or ground. Terriers were developed as "earth dogs" that dig and burrow after their small prey.) Other groups are Herding, Toy, and Non-Sporting (Again, an explanation is in order. The Non-Sporting Group is a hodge-podge, the organization of which defies explanation. It is an interesting mix of breeds as varied as the uses for which they were intended.)

If the characteristics of one of these groups appeal to you and fit in with your family's lifestyle and your kids' personalities and preferences, learn more about breeds within that group until you narrow your choices down to two or three to research carefully before making that final cut.

Above all, use your judgment. If you follow these guidelines for selecting the perfect dog for your kids, you'll be way ahead of the game and so will the dog— especially if you are a first-time dog owner.

The AKC recognizes 141 breeds. There are also hundreds of other breeds around the world, not to mention the infinite variety of All-American mixed breeds, a.k.a. mutts. It's a mind-boggling choice for the first-time dog owner.

These summaries include discriptions of one, two or three breeds that are good choices for a family with kids. They're only the beginning.

SPORTING GROUP

It would be almost impossible to find a well-bred Sporting dog that does not make an excellent companion for an active family. This is true probably because Sporting dogs were bred to be easily trained and worked in the field. The various pointers, retrievers, setters and spaniels that make up the group were developed to hunt birds by working in cooperation with people. They like being with and learning from their human companions. Active outdoor dogs, they need a good daily workout, after which they're ready for dinner and a nap by the fire. They need regular grooming and a thorough check for burrs and ticks after a day outdoors.

Sporting breeds are: American Water Spaniel, Brittany, Chesapeake Bay Retriever, Clumber Spaniel, Cocker Spaniel, Curly-Coated

Sporting dogs are easily trained and thrive with a lot of outdoor activity and exercise. A Chesapeake Bay Retriever.

Working breeds are devoted pals and guardians. Karina and Chantel Massey with a St. Bernard puppy.

park where he can go flat out.

The most famous Frisbee™-catching dog ever was Ashley Whippet, a gravity-defying canine superstar who captured three Frisbee disc-catching world titles and gave his name to the Ashley Whippet Invitational, since renamed the Alpo Canine Frisbee Disc Championships, and the Ashley Whippet Hall of Fame for top dogs in that sport. Ashley had his own attorney, a credit card in his name, and an ice cream store named after him.

Another popular sport for sighthounds is lure coursing, a great outdoor family sport that tests sighthounds on their abilities to hunt down prey by sight. In this case, the prey is a plastic bag pulled at high speed along a guide wire powered by a mechanical device. The dogs tear after the lure and are judged on their overall ability, speed, agility, endurance and how closely they track the lure. Their owners cheer them on and then everyone enjoys a tailgate picnic. Your kid's dog will have the best of both worlds.

WORKING GROUP

Most breeds in this group are large and know how to think for themselves, because they have been developed to perform work that requires them to do just that—driving cattle, guarding families and livestock, fighting beside warriors, and pulling carts and heavy loads. Working dogs need to have a job to do and someone to tell them to

do it. If you don't tell a Working dog what you want him to do, he'll consider you a wimp and decide that he is the boss. As you can imagine, this can cause the human-canine bond to deteriorate rapidly. Obedience training is a must.

Most Working breeds are not for first-time dog owners.

However, if you are experienced in training and socializing these breeds and are willing to take the time to teach your kids, a Working dog can be a devoted companion and guardian.

Working breeds are: Akita, Alaskan Malamute, Bernese Mountain Dog, Boxer, Bullmastiff, Doberman Pinscher, Giant Schnauzer, Great Dane, Great Pyrenees, Greater Swiss Mountain Dog, Komondor, Kuvasz, Mastiff, Newfoundland, Portuguese Water Dog, Rottweiler, Saint Bernard, Samoyed, Siberian Husky and Standard Schnauzer.

The gentle Newfoundland is happiest near the water. Bonnie Hoye and her Newfie, Inky.

in that group have similar characteristics. The group names are self-explanatory: Sporting, Hound, Working, Terrier (It helps if you know a little Latin. Terrier comes from *terra* , Latin for earth or ground. Terriers were developed as "earth dogs" that dig and burrow after their small prey.) Other groups are Herding, Toy, and Non-Sporting (Again, an explanation is in order. The Non-Sporting Group is a hodge-podge, the organization of which defies explanation. It is an interesting mix of breeds as varied as the uses for which they were intended.)

If the characteristics of one of these groups appeal to you and fit in with your family's lifestyle and your kids' personalities and preferences, learn more about breeds within that group until you narrow your choices down to two or three to research carefully before making that final cut.

Above all, use your judgment. If you follow these guidelines for selecting the perfect dog for your kids, you'll be way ahead of the game and so will the dog—especially if you are a first-time dog owner.

The AKC recognizes 141 breeds. There are also hundreds of other breeds around the world, not to mention the infinite variety of All-American mixed breeds, a.k.a. mutts. It's a mind-boggling choice for the first-time dog owner.

These summaries include discriptions of one, two or three breeds that are good choices for a family with kids. They're only the beginning.

SPORTING GROUP

It would be almost impossible to find a well-bred Sporting dog that does not make an excellent companion for an active family. This is true probably because Sporting dogs were bred to be easily trained and worked in the field. The various pointers, retrievers, setters and spaniels that make up the group were developed to hunt birds by working in cooperation with people. They like being with and learning from their human companions. Active outdoor dogs, they need a good daily workout, after which they're ready for dinner and a nap by the fire. They need regular grooming and a thorough check for burrs and ticks after a day outdoors.

Sporting breeds are: American Water Spaniel, Brittany, Chesapeake Bay Retriever, Clumber Spaniel, Cocker Spaniel, Curly-Coated

Sporting dogs are easily trained and thrive with a lot of outdoor activity and exercise. A Chesapeake Bay Retriever.

Retriever, English Cocker Spaniel, English Setter, English Springer Spaniel, Field Spaniel, Flat-Coated Retriver, German Shorthaired Pointer, German Wirehaired Pointer, Golden Retriever, Gordon Setter, Irish Setter, Irish Water Spaniel, Labrador Retriever, Pointer, Sussex Spaniel, Vizsla, Weimaraner, Welsh Springer Spaniel and Wirehaired Pointing Griffon.

Labrador Retriever

Whether he's black, chocolate or mellow yellow, the easy-going Lab is America's most popular purebred dog. Whatever his family does is all right with him. He loves children of all ages. He's sizeable and strong, but when he's well-trained, he makes the best companion and teammate imaginable. He's eager to learn and loves to work. Just keep in mind: That adorable little furball will grow to be 70 pounds. Grooming is minimal, but baths are in order.

If your family enjoys being in and around the water, the Lab is a perfect choice. Originally bred for field huntng and water retrieving, he's happy swimming and water-retrieving balls, sticks and kids all day long. He's a great all-round family dog and will enthusiastically join in any and all of your kids' activities.

English Springer Spaniel

A good mid-size teammate and family companion is this outgoing fellow, bred to be your kid's best friend. Your Springer's fondest wish is that he always be by your side. The person who loves him, feeds him, trains him and plays with him will have a constant, faithful companion for life. He'll look at you as if you're the center of his universe, as indeed you are. There's no more soulful

A friend until the end, the English Springer Spaniel enjoys nothing more than being with his loved ones.

expression in all dogdom.

He's jolly, fun-loving and eager to please. Bred to be a versatile hunter, he enjoys tracking, retrieving and swimming. He learns quickly and retains what you teach him.

He's sturdy, compact and athletic; as ready to spring after a Frisbee as a pheasant. His coat is silky, medium-length, liver and white or black and white. It requires regular brushing. After a day outside, it also probably needs a thorough going-over for ticks and burrs. Some hand-trimming is needed to keep the throat, feet and ears looking their best.

The Springer is happiest in the suburbs or country where there's room for him to run and frolic. If there's swimming nearby, so much the better!

Golden Retriever

With a disposition as sunny as the color of his beautiful golden coat, the Golden is a

The easy-going Labrador Retriever is one of the most popular family breeds.

favorite family dog. He's good with kids of all ages, and can be a trustworthy guardian to small children. Because of his size and strength, however, younger children will need an adult's help with his training and on-lead exercise.

This breed is intelligent, easy to train and willing to perform. Many top winners in agility and obedience are Goldens. They are used as guide dogs for the blind, hearing dogs for the deaf, and therapy dogs in nursing homes and hospitals.

The well-bred Golden is healthy and robust. However, hip dysplasia has been a hereditary problem in the breed, so purchase your Golden from a reputable breeder, who will provide you with health certification.

HOUND GROUP

The Hounds, including Beagles like Jimmy Banegas, were developed to track down game for their owners. To work successfully with hunters, they had to be good-natured, easily trainable and eager to please. They also had to have a strong inbred desire to hunt. Some hounds tend to be independent and even stubborn, because they have been bred to work on their own and, once they are on the scent, will follow it whether you want them to or not. Because they lived together in kennels and hunted in packs, they are sociable creatures and get along well with other dogs and humans.

Hounds are divided into two types, the scenthound and the sighthound or gazehound. Scenthounds include these breeds: American Foxhound, Basset

Hound, Beagle, Black and Tan Coonhound, Bloodhound, Dachshund, English Foxhound, Harrier, Otterhound and Petit Basset Griffon Vendeen.

The hounds in this category use their noses to track and hunt down small game such as rabbits, foxes, otter and raccoons. Some breeds, such as Beagles and Bassets, are built close to the ground, the better to hunt ground-dwelling prey. Domestic cats and hamsters, beware!

Foxhounds have long, strong legs that take them wherever the fox goes—over uneven ground, over fences, uphill and down. The Otterhound has a full double coat to keep him warm as he plunges into icy water after

Scenthounds, like this Bloodhound, have an inherent desire to use their noses to hunt game.

Dogs that belong in the Hound group are good-natured, trainable and eager to please. This Dachshund is a welcome part of the family.

Working breeds are devoted pals and guardians. Karina and Chantel Massey with a St. Bernard puppy.

park where he can go flat out.

The most famous Frisbee™-catching dog ever was Ashley Whippet, a gravity-defying canine superstar who captured three Frisbee disc-catching world titles and gave his name to the Ashley Whippet Invitational, since renamed the Alpo Canine Frisbee Disc Championships, and the Ashley Whippet Hall of Fame for top dogs in that sport. Ashley had his own attorney, a credit card in his name, and an ice cream store named after him.

Another popular sport for sighthounds is lure coursing, a great outdoor family sport that tests sighthounds on their abilities to hunt down prey by sight. In this case, the prey is a plastic bag pulled at high speed along a guide wire powered by a mechanical device. The dogs tear after the lure and are judged on their overall ability, speed, agility, endurance and how closely they track the lure. Their owners cheer them on and then everyone enjoys a tailgate picnic. Your kid's dog will have the best of both worlds.

WORKING GROUP

Most breeds in this group are large and know how to think for themselves, because they have been developed to perform work that requires them to do just that—driving cattle, guarding families and livestock, fighting beside warriors, and pulling carts and heavy loads. Working dogs need to have a job to do and someone to tell them to

do it. If you don't tell a Working dog what you want him to do, he'll consider you a wimp and decide that he is the boss. As you can imagine, this can cause the human-canine bond to deteriorate rapidly. Obedience training is a must.

Most Working breeds are not for first-time dog owners.

However, if you are experienced in training and socializing these breeds and are willing to take the time to teach your kids, a Working dog can be a devoted companion and guardian.

Working breeds are: Akita, Alaskan Malamute, Bernese Mountain Dog, Boxer, Bullmastiff, Doberman Pinscher, Giant Schnauzer, Great Dane, Great Pyrenees, Greater Swiss Mountain Dog, Komondor, Kuvasz, Mastiff, Newfoundland, Portuguese Water Dog, Rottweiler, Saint Bernard, Samoyed, Siberian Husky and Standard Schnauzer.

The gentle Newfoundland is happiest near the water. Bonnie Hoye and her Newfie, Inky.

favorite family dog. He's good with kids of all ages, and can be a trustworthy guardian to small children. Because of his size and strength, however, younger children will need an adult's help with his training and on-lead exercise.

This breed is intelligent, easy to train and willing to perform. Many top winners in agility and obedience are Goldens. They are used as guide dogs for the blind, hearing dogs for the deaf, and therapy dogs in nursing homes and hospitals.

The well-bred Golden is healthy and robust. However, hip dysplasia has been a hereditary problem in the breed, so purchase your Golden from a reputable breeder, who will provide you with health certification.

HOUND GROUP

The Hounds, including Beagles like Jimmy Banegas, were developed to track down game for their owners. To work successfully with hunters, they had to be good-natured, easily trainable and eager to please. They also had to have a strong inbred desire to hunt. Some hounds tend to be independent and even stubborn, because they have been bred to work on their own and, once they are on the scent, will follow it whether you want them to or not. Because they lived together in kennels and hunted in packs, they are sociable creatures and get along well with other dogs and humans.

Hounds are divided into two types, the scenthound and the sighthound or gazehound. Scenthounds include these breeds: American Foxhound, Basset Hound, Beagle, Black and Tan Coonhound, Bloodhound, Dachshund, English Foxhound, Harrier, Otterhound and Petit Basset Griffon Vendeen.

The hounds in this category use their noses to track and hunt down small game such as rabbits, foxes, otter and raccoons. Some breeds, such as Beagles and Bassets, are built close to the ground, the better to hunt ground-dwelling prey. Domestic cats and hamsters, beware!

Foxhounds have long, strong legs that take them wherever the fox goes—over uneven ground, over fences, uphill and down. The Otterhound has a full double coat to keep him warm as he plunges into icy water after

Scenthounds, like this Bloodhound, have an inherent desire to use their noses to hunt game.

Dogs that belong in the Hound group are good-natured, trainable and eager to please. This Dachshund is a welcome part of the family.

his prey, the aquatic otter.

Hounds can be versatile hunters, tracking anything that moves and has a scent. For example, although Dachshunds usually hunt small game that lives in underground burrows, some of these little earthdogs are even used to track animals as large as deer. When scenthounds locate prey, they let their handlers know by "giving voice"—some with musical baying, others with a sharp bark. Hounds do love the sound of their own voices, so if a hound who likes to seranade your neighbors is your choice, be prepared to distract him with a game of Gumabone® Frisbee™. It

youngsters to handle.

Because sighthounds love to run, they must be kept on a lead when not in the house or in an enclosed area. It's best if you live near a large fenced schoolyard or dog park where they can exercise by doing what they love best— running flat out.

Sighthounds are bred to cover ground independently, without constant direction from their handlers. Therefore, they can be stubborn and aloof, not the best choice for a family seeking a well-trained house dog that responds readily to commands.

Sighthounds are: Afghan Hound, Basenji, Borzoi,

Beagle can really cover ground. He needs plenty of exercise.

For smaller children, the 13-inch variety of this breed is ideal. The 15-inch Beagle would be a good choice for older kids. Beagle colors are usually tan, black and white, and need only occasional brushing. Sociable dogs, they get along well with kids, adults and other dogs. But small pets beware! The Beagle's hunting instinct tells him they are prey.

Beagles are quick! Never forget that this is a dog with tracking in his blood. Before you open a door, know exactly where your Beagle is. Check your backyard fence every day for gaps and hot-diggedy-dog escape holes.

They're delightful little beggars at table and will eat until they pop, so steel yourself. An obese Beagle is at risk for any number of health problems.

Some Beagles tend to have a stubborn streak, so be prepared to establish your authority. If you start training early and are consistent, you will have a well-behaved, affectionate, loyal, adorable low-maintenance family pet.

A playful, friendly breed, the Beagle has been a first choice for families for years. Abby Banegas and Jimmy are ready to play.

helps to have dog-loving neighbors who understand the ways of the canine companion.

Sighthounds, the swiftest of all dogs, locate quarry with their keen eyes. They possess speed and stamina, for they were bred to chase game sometimes as large as deer, wolves and even lions over the ground. The large, very strong breeds, originally intended to attack and kill large game, are loyal protectors of home and children, but a bit much for

Greyhound, Ibizan Hound, Irish Wolfhound, Norwegian Elkhound, Pharaoh Hound, Rhodesian Ridgeback, Saluki, Scottish Deerhound and Whippet.

Beagle

Jimmy the Beagle, a scenthound, is the perfect choice for the Banegas family, and might be for yours. This playful, friendly breed is good with kids who enjoy outdoor activities, because although he is small in stature, the

Basset Hound

The low-slung Basset is another sweetheart in the Hound group. He's small enough not to bowl over small children in play and sturdy enough to withstand vigorous activity. He's also gentle, loyal and loving, and can be a delightful clown. Like the Beagle, he's an avid hunter with an exceptionally keen sense of smell. Covering ground at a slow, determined pace, he is a formidable adversary to rabbit and larger game. With loud, melodious baying, he lets his his handler know he's on the track.

He loves to be outdoors in all weather and on all terrain, and will cheerfully leave muddy tracks throughout the house if you are not ready with an old towel.

Because of his inbred instinct to hunt independently of regular commands, he tends to be independent. But if you and your kids are patient, consistent trainers, he will be a well-behaved, loyal and loving companion.

Bassets love to trundle over field and meadow on long walks, but not all athletic pursuits are right for these short-legged fellows. If Agility appeals to your kids, ask them to picture a Basset gamely maneuvering his length over a steep-sided A-frame obstacle or climbing over, rather than jumping, a fence.

Greyhound and Whippet

The Greyhound and the smaller Whippet are good choices as family pets because of their gentle nature, ability to adapt to confinement in house or apartment, and inclination to be a companionable couch potato as well as an outdoor athlete. Buy your dog from a reputable breeder, or consider adopting a retired racing dog. Because these dogs have a short "professional" life and then face an uncertain future unless they are adopted, there is never a shortage of Greyhounds and Whippets available to loving adoptive families.

Because he's never known any life other than running in

A Whippet is a good choice for a child's pet because of his gentle nature and his ability to adapt to any situation.

races and being kept in close confinement when not on the track, the adopted sighthound will have a period of adjustment to his new life. He'll probably prefer to be in his crate, and your kid will have to be patient in coaxing him out and persuading him

it's all right to be one of the family.

A fence around your property is essential if you're planning to get a dog, especially a dog that lives to run. Your sighthound must be exercised regularly. Try to find a fenced schoolyard or dog

Working breeds are devoted pals and guardians. Karina and Chantel Massey with a St. Bernard puppy.

park where he can go flat out.

The most famous Frisbee™-catching dog ever was Ashley Whippet, a gravity-defying canine superstar who captured three Frisbee disc-catching world titles and gave his name to the Ashley Whippet Invitational, since renamed the Alpo Canine Frisbee Disc Championships, and the Ashley Whippet Hall of Fame for top dogs in that sport. Ashley had his own attorney, a credit card in his name, and an ice cream store named after him.

Another popular sport for sighthounds is lure coursing, a great outdoor family sport that tests sighthounds on their abilities to hunt down prey by sight. In this case, the prey is a plastic bag pulled at high speed along a guide wire powered by a mechanical device. The dogs tear after the lure and are judged on their overall ability, speed, agility, endurance and how closely they track the lure. Their owners cheer them on and then everyone enjoys a tailgate picnic. Your kid's dog will have the best of both worlds.

WORKING GROUP

Most breeds in this group are large and know how to think for themselves, because they have been developed to perform work that requires them to do just that—driving cattle, guarding families and livestock, fighting beside warriors, and pulling carts and heavy loads. Working dogs need to have a job to do and someone to tell them to do it. If you don't tell a Working dog what you want him to do, he'll consider you a wimp and decide that he is the boss. As you can imagine, this can cause the human-canine bond to deteriorate rapidly. Obedience training is a must.

Most Working breeds are not for first-time dog owners.

However, if you are experienced in training and socializing these breeds and are willing to take the time to teach your kids, a Working dog can be a devoted companion and guardian.

Working breeds are: Akita, Alaskan Malamute, Bernese Mountain Dog, Boxer, Bullmastiff, Doberman Pinscher, Giant Schnauzer, Great Dane, Great Pyrenees, Greater Swiss Mountain Dog, Komondor, Kuvasz, Mastiff, Newfoundland, Portuguese Water Dog, Rottweiler, Saint Bernard, Samoyed, Siberian Husky and Standard Schnauzer.

The gentle Newfoundland is happiest near the water. Bonnie Hoye and her Newfie, Inky.

Newfoundland

Betty Bonora wanted a large dog that would be gentle with her daughter, and at the same time intimidate unwelcome strangers. She chose a Newf—big, black, lovable Inky, appropriately named by newspaper (or is it newfspaper?) editor Bonora.

Originally bred to help fishermen haul heavy nets, pull carts and carry loads in big bags, Newfs also bravely carried out rescues at sea, braving storm-tossed waters to carry lines to sailors in distress and swimming with them to shore.

Newfs love children, open spaces and water. Inky is a happy dog with Betty's daughter Bonnie and his miles of beach and ocean on the East End of Long Island, New York.

The Newf coat, usually black but sometimes brown, gray or black-and-white, should be brushed every day, especially during shedding season. "Also," says Bonora, "they drool." Because of their size, obedience training is essential. They're too strong for a young child to handle,

but an ideal family dog if the tot has an older sibling.

TERRIER GROUP

At 25 breeds, this is the largest group, ranging in size from the scrappy little Cairn Terrier to the large Airedale and in structure from the slender, elegant Manchester Terrier to the stocky Bull Terrier breeds. Some terriers are earthdogs, bred to hunt and kill burrowing vermin such as rats, badgers, foxes and weasels. Built for chasing and digging, they are hardy, well-muscled dogs with strong bones and courageous natures. Inveterate busybodies, they are fun-loving companions, always game for a romp. Their bold, independent nature often prompts them to go in one direction when you want them to go in another, so you'll need to be consistently firm but gentle in training.

Other terriers, such as the American Staffordshire Terrier, Bull Terrier and Staffordshire Bull Terrier, were originally bred as fighting dogs. Although they are sweet-tempered and

Dogs in the Terrier group, like this Yorkshire Terrier, are independent, fun loving and hardy pets for children.

affectionate, they need an experienced owner who knows how to be firm-handed yet gentle in handling.

Some terriers need expert grooming; others have low-maintenance coats. Don't tempt their strong hunting instincts by leaving them alone with small pets.

Terriers are: Airedale Terrier, American Staffordshire Terrier, Australian Terrier, Bedlington Terrier, Border Terrier, Bull Terrier, Cairn Terrier, Dandie Dinmont Terrier, Fox Terrier (Smooth), Fox Terrier (Wire), Irish Terrier, Kerry Blue Terrier, Lakeland Terrier, Manchester Terrier, Miniature Bull Terrier, Miniature Schnauzer, Norfolk Terrier, Norwich Terrier, Scottish Terrier, Sealyham Terrier, Skye Terrier, Soft Coated Wheaten Terrier, Staffordshire

Two-year-old Cassie Timmsen and her Boxer, Magic, do everything together!

The Fox Terrier is an eager, alert dog that needs lots of exercise. Lena O'Keefe is ready to play ball with her Smooth Fox Terrier.

His markings are rich rust on a glossy black short coat. The two rust spots over his eyes are called "kiss marks," your kids will kiss them often.

A small variety of this breed, the Toy Manchester Terrier, is a member of the Toy Group.

Smooth and Wire Fox Terriers

These alert, eager terriers, once classified as varieties within a breed, are now considered two separate breeds. Like other terriers, both were developed to hunt and go to ground after fox and other small animals that preyed upon poultry and ate feed meant for livestock. Tails a-quiver, they are hardy, curious, smart and playful. If not exercised regularly to take the edge off their seemingly boundless energy, their inquisitive nature might get them into mischief. Long walks are their favorite activity.

The Wire Fox Terrier has a sharper, more spirited presence than the Smooth Fox Terrier, who can be more of a gentleman. Both breeds are good with children and enjoy sounding the alarm if an unknown person or dog approaches the house. They are fine Canine Good Citizens and keen competitors in Obedience or Conformation.

The Smooth, which sheds twice a year, requires very little grooming. The Wire's thicker coat—a crinkly top coat and soft undercoat—needs combing and brushing at least twice weekly and stripping twice a year to remove its old dead coat.

TOY GROUP

Some Toys were originally

Bull Terrier, Welsh Terrier and West Highland White Terrier.

Manchester Terrier

This sleek breed has been refined over the years from a cross between the tough Black and Tan Terrier—an old British breed—and the quick, agile Whippet. An excellent watch dog, he will become deeply devoted to your family, if a bit standoffish with strangers, and is happy at home in the country or city. He's good with children and usually gets along with other dogs. He's big enough for strenuous exercise and small enough for your kid to pick up and cuddle. Nimble and athletic, he enjoys Agility and is a quick learner.

bred as watch dogs, others as ratters, and almost all as companions. They're portable, cuddly, adorable and love to play, but because of their size, children must be taught to handle them with care.

They can live almost anywhere, from estate to apartment, and are a good choice for the family that prefers indoor activities to outdoor rough-and-tumble. Some Toys are keen competitors in obedience and agility. Most make delightful pets for all ages.

Toy dogs are: Affenpinscher, Brussels Griffon, Cavalier King Charles Spaniel, Chihuahua, Chinese Crested, English Toy Spaniel, Italian Greyhound, Japanese Chin, Maltese, Manchester Terrier (Toy), Miniature Pinscher, Papillon, Pekingese, Pomeranian, Poodle (Toy), Pug, Shih Tzu, Silky Terrier and Yorkshire Terrier.

Miniature Pinscher

The Min Pin loves children and is an excellent choice for kids who will treat this small dog with gentleness and respect. He was originally bred as a companion, watch dog and ratter, and he is equally happy snuggling in your lap, barking at strangers, or racing around outside chasing squirrels or leaping over Agility obstacles.

Known as the "King of Toys," the Min Pin has an attitude that says, "Look at me!" Dressed in a low-maintenance black and rust, clear red, stag red (red interspersed with black), or chocolate and rust coat, he is a big dog in a small package. A highly intelligent dog, he can be independent, and

Miniature Pinschers and other Toy breeds require gentle treatment and will love a child who understands respect.

training sometimes requires an extra measure of patience, consistency and perseverance —which is rewarded with a charming, lively companion. He loves to show off and is especially adept at performing clever tricks, pulling

miniature carts and walking on his hind legs.

Papillon

An excellent obedience and agility dog, the Pap is a sweet companion to kids who know how to treat the little guys. *Papillon*, the French word for butterfly, gives him his name because of his butterfly-wing ears. His long, silky coat is white with patches of black. His agreeable temperament and trainability probably result from his origins in Spain as a miniature spaniel.

The Pap makes an affectionate, elegant companion for the city family. He is also a hardy teammate for the youngster who enjoys outdoor sports.

NON-SPORTING DOGS

This is the mixed-bag group of breeds that apparently couldn't be categorized anywhere else. And what an interesting group it is! Here

The Papillion is an excellent athlete that also possesses an affectionate and agreeable temperament.

Although the Dalmatian was once bred to be a coach dog, today he is more likely to be found on a fire engine than leading one!

The Non-Sporting breeds have evolved from working dogs into companions. With no snow or sleds around, these two American Eskimo dogs are happy to be lap dogs.

Bulldog, Keeshond, Lhasa Apso, Poodle (Standard and Miniature), Schipperke, Shiba Inu, Tibetan Spaniel and Tibetan Terrier.

Boston Terrier
This spiffy-looking black-and-white dog is a true all-

A truly "all-American" dog, the Boston Terrier is an intelligent dog who enjoys the company of children.

you'll find the Poodle, which was originally a retriever—a sporting dog. The Boston Terrier is not a Terrier, nor is he a Toy, although he is small enough to be included in that group. The Dalmatian was once a coach dog; the Keeshond and Schipperke boat dogs. The Lhasa Apso was a watch dog for monasteries high in the mountains of Tibet.

Today, the Non-Sporting dogs usually don't perform the tasks for which they were originally bred. Their primary purpose is to be companions. They enjoy being with people and usually are quick to learn and eager to join in family activities.

The Non-Sporting breeds are: American Eskimo Dog, Bichon Frise, Boston Terrier, Bulldog, Chinese Shar-Pei, Chow Chow, Dalmatian, Finnish Spitz, French

Herding dogs are natural baby-sitters and loyal pets. Katie Kennedy is best friends with her Australian Shepherd, Chester.

American. The breed was developed in Boston during the late 1800s by crossing English and French Bulldogs and a white English terrier. Maybe Boston University thinks the little dog looks fierce; he is the mascot of BU's football team. Although his two main ancestors were fighting dogs, the little Boston is an affectionate companion and loves to snuggle. He likes children and gets along well with other pets. Highly intelligent, he is good at obedience and loves to perform tricks.

HERDING DOGS

Nimble and quick, these farmers' and shepherds' right-hand dogs were developed to control the movements of herds of livestock. They are highly intelligent and have a strong inborn need to work. They are loyal to their owners, and look to them for instruction in what to do. If you don't give them a job, they'll go to work on the furniture or herd children and pets around the house and yard.

Herding dogs are always busy. Recently at an agility match, I saw a Border Collie who didn't think events were moving along quickly enough for him. He decided to herd the woman standing in front of him and took a nip at her broad backside.

Some Herding breeds serve as police dogs, guard dogs and guide dogs for the blind. Most are quick to learn and easy to train in obedience. They are also enthusiastic agility athletes. Full of energy and the desire to work, they need to be exercised regularly and often.

Collie

Thanks to the Lassie of story, movie and television, the elegant, luxuriant-coated Rough Collie is today a popular family dog. The breed was developed in northern England and Scotland to herd sheep, and like all working breeds, the Collie needs lots of activity to stay well-behaved and happy.

The Collie is gregarious. He loves kids and gets along well with other dogs. He thrives on activity, and will play for hours at Flyball, Frisbee and Agility.

One of his outstanding features is his thick, full coat. Be prepared to brush it daily, all the way down to the skin, or it will become messy and matted.

MISCELLANEOUS CLASS AND RARE BREEDS

In addition to these designated breed groups, the AKC has created a Miscellaneous Class, comprised of breeds recognized elsewhere in the world, but not yet by the AKC. These breeds can participate in AKC obedience trials and earn titles. Also, they can compete in the Miscellaneous Class at conformation shows, but are ineligible to earn championship points. When a breed is well established over time in the United States as healthy and consistent in temperament, structure, movement and other qualities standardized by the breed club, it may gain AKC recognition.

Miscellaneous Class breeds are: Anatolian Shepherd Dog, Australian Kelpie, Canaan Dog, Havanese, Lowchen and Spinone Italiano. Hundreds of breeds exist throughout the world. Some are designated "rare breeds" and have names like Steinbracke, Small Gascony Blue, Treeing Tennessee Brindle and Peruvian Inca Orchid, to cite a few. These rarities have loyal fanciers who sponsor shows and maintain bloodlines.

Ownership of these breeds, many of which are still being developed toward an American standard, should be left to the experienced breeder and exhibitor. There are so many family-friendly breeds that have been developed over hundreds of years for stable temperament and other desirable qualities, that you'll have challenge enough

choosing the perfect dog for your kid without further complicating the process.

ALL-AMERICAN (MIXED BREED)

If left to their own devices, say some experts on canine genetics, dogs that breed indiscriminately without benefit of human planning eventually take on the appearance of the Pariah, a prototype dog that originated in the Middle East and migrated throughout Asia before recorded history. Many strays and "junkyard dogs" that have been whelped for generations in alleyways and

forests have the street-wise, alert expression, erect ears, long tail, medium size and athletic build of their canine cousins the wolf and coyote or of the "Carolina Dog," a straw-colored breed that occurs in the Deep South and that fanciers claim is a direct descendent of the original Pariah.

Then there are the All-American pooches who look like something out of a Norman Rockwell painting. A terrier-spaniel cross? A shepherd-pinscher amalgam? The purebreds who are abandoned or relinquished to

A mixed breed can make an excellent pet. Theresa Power and Spanky, her mixed breed pal.

Every breed, and every puppy within a breed, has a personality all its own.

shelters by their owners have their champions in the breed rescue organizations. But who will stand up for the homeless mixed-breed?

Fortunately, shelters increasingly make every effort to find new homes for all dogs in their care. If, after studying the type of dog you like, you decide to give a homeless All-American a new lease on life, you might be able to find one that closely approximates the breed you prefer, with a little of something-or-another thrown in for what mutt-fanciers call "hybrid vigor."

But be careful. When you adopt an All-American, you risk inheriting someone else's breeding and behavioral mistakes. Be prepared for a period of adjustment. With understanding, patience, gentle firmness, and the occasional phone call to your veterinarian, trainer and doggy friends, you could find that you have a diamond in the ruff.

Mixed breeds compete and excel in flyball, Frisbee™, most agility competition and many other sports and activities. They can be the most loyal, affectionate companions for kids and the very best friends of all.

Mixed breeds can participate with children in many activities, including agility. This Chow-Sheltie mix flies over the wall jump.

The time you want to spend on grooming should be a consideration when selecting a breed. These two well-groomed girls are ready for a night on the town!

CHOOSING THE RIGHT BREEDER

"Money will buy a pretty good dog, but it won't buy the wag of his tail." — *Josh Billings*

You've decided on a breed you like and the hunt is on—for a puppy! When a pup is eight weeks old, it is weaned, vaccinated and is ready to your new family member. Try to plan the pup purchase for a school vacation, when your kids can be at home to help the baby puppy adapt to her new surroundings.

An experienced, knowledgeable breeder is the very best source for a well-crisis arises, you'll have someone to turn to, for the conscientious breeder considers each of his pups family for life.

When you're ready, approach breeders who, with their dogs, have impressed you favorably at shows, or

A reputable breeder will produce healthy, well socialized puppies. Boxer puppies bred by Rick Tomita.

bond with a lifetime human companion. The most important time in a dog's life is between eight and ten weeks. Because the impressions the pup receives during this fleeting time will stay with her the rest of her life, be prepared to take some time off to devote full attention to loving, caring, and gently beginning to train bred, healthy dog or puppy. Serious breeders are committed to improving the breed and expect to do so with each new litter. Also, a reputable breeder won't wave good-bye, shut the door and forget all about you as soon as he's made a sale. He'll expect to hear from you with questions, especially if you are a first-time dog owner. If a who have been recommended by the local or national breed club. If you don't already know breeders or someone in a club who can recommend them, get the name of the national breed club secretary from the American Kennel Club. The club secretary will send you the names of breeders in your area.

Ask each breeder when the

Find a conscientious breeder who is committed to improving the breed and finding good homes for all his dogs. Martha Shepherd with her pet Poodle.

next litter is due. Most reputable breeders will not plan a litter until they have a good home lined up for each pup.

Make appointments ahead of time. When visiting breeders, ask about each individual pup and

temperament test? Are his or her dogs good with children?

4. The dam (mother)—If you're buying a puppy, ask to see the dam. This will give you an idea of what your pup will be like as an adult. Ask to see other dogs from the same bloodline.

The way a puppy relates to his littermates will tell you a lot about his personality.

Your pup will have a head start in life if his parents are healthy and well adjusted. If possible, meet the dam of the puppy you are considering. A Great Dane mom and her pups.

characteristics of the breed. Don't be shy. If you don't ask thoughtful questions, the breeder might hesitate to place one of her precious pups in your care. Note if the breeder is knowledgeable and enthusiastic as you ask about:

1. His or her experience as a breeder.

2. How many litters a year does he or she breed? (Responsible breeders plan carefully. This means that less is more.)

3. Temperament—Has the breeder administered a

5. Characteristics of the breed.

6. Problems in the breed.

7. Accomplishments of parents and others in same line—How many champions? Obedience titles? Other titles?

8. Health considerations: Have both parents been x-rayed and certified free of hip dysplasia? Have they been tested for heartworm and other parasites?

9. Medical history of the litter.

10. Spay-neuter contract.

11. Proper nutrition.

12. Ask about a health guarantee. The breeder should offer a full refund if any health problems turn up in a veterinarian examination within 48 hours.

13. Ask to see the pups' pedigree. This is a family tree showing three or more generations of the litter's ancestors. The breeder can tell you something about Grandma and Granddad, brag a little about the stars in the puppies' background. He'll show you photos, so he can point out the attributes of some of the litter's forebears.

Take a tip from Jimmy the Beagle: Use your nose! Sniff as you walk through the breeder's house and kennel.

Curiosity may have killed the cat, but it never hurt a Weimaraner! The puppy you choose should be bright-eyed, responsive and interested in the world around him.

Does it smell clean? Are the puppies clean, well fed, lively and friendly? Are they free from signs of illness such as runny nose and eyes, sores, dirty or foul-smelling ears? Use your eyes, too. Do you see any ticks or fleas?

Look around the breeder's house or "dog room." Does a display of rosettes, trophies and photos indicate that this breeder has a history of commitment to the breed?

Notice how littermates act with each other, the breeder and you. Now's the time to put into practice your self-analysis and match the pup to your family. Do you want a submissive, quiet type or a bold and brassy show-off? In every litter is an alpha pup who will bowl over the others, grab the toys and be the first to approach you with curiosity and kisses. If your youngster has a high energy level as well as a strong personality and will have no trouble showing a dog who is boss, this outgoing, energetic dynamo is the pup for you.

Then there's the Number 2 dog, lively and intelligent, who will be full of fun, but easier to train than somewhat willful Number 1. And so on down to the shyest of the litter. This may be a sweet little fellow who just isn't as assertive as the others. He may be just the right companion for a shy, quiet child. On the other hand, if this little underdog is timid and cringing, he could develop into a fear biter or display other behavioral problems later on. If he is listless, he might be a shrinking violet all his life, and you'll spend years feeling sorry for him.

Pick up each pup and test him or her for dominance and submission. Turn the pup belly-up. The most dominant one will struggle and even bite to escape. No. 2 will wriggle and eventually right himself, shake and trot off. No. 3 will lie there and happily submit to a tummy rub. No. 4 will just lie there. You don't want to see negative reactions such as whimpering, crying in fright, or excessive biting (It's normal for puppies to do some mouthing or nibbling until you train them not to.)

Discuss with the breeder the pros and cons of each

When you visit a breeder, make sure the facilities are clean and the puppies are happy, healthy and well cared for.

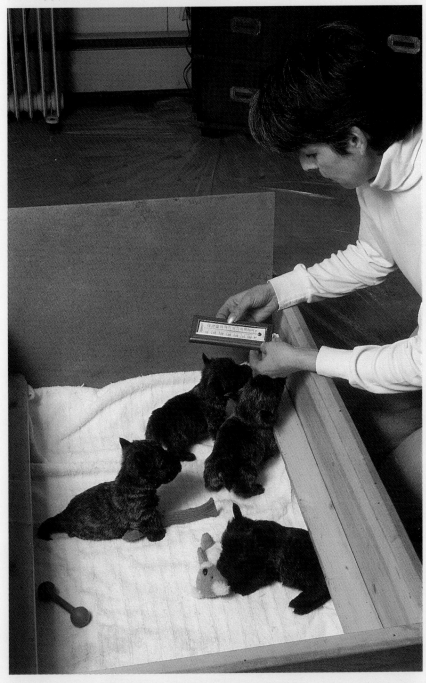

Last out is a rotten egg! The dominant pup will be evident this basketful of Labrador Retrievers.

pup. She or he has been observing them for eight or more weeks, and will mention things you will have missed.

Breeders usually screen prospective owners just as carefully as you should screen your puppy's "first Mom or Dad." Don't be insulted if the breeder quizzes you on such

When these Shetland Sheepdogs are old enough to leave their mother, their breeder will make sure they go to good homes.

topics as your own knowledge of dogs and the breed, your lifestyle, whether your yard is fenced, what kind of training or handling you plan for the pup and whether someone will be home during the day. She just wants to know her pup will be in good hands.

If you purchase a show-quality pup, be prepared to pay top dollar, an amount that varies among breeds and breeders. If you don't plan to finish your dog to a championship in conformation shows, you can still get a beautiful purebred "pet-quality" pup that will look every bit the champion to anyone other than an experienced breeder or judge — at a fraction of the cost of his show-quality littermate. He will be qualified to compete in obedience trials, agility, lure coursing, field trials, and all aspects of the sport except conformation. Your child can still handle him in Junior Showmanship.

Together, you can train him for Canine Good Citizen certification or simply as a well-mannered beloved family pet.

Nevertheless, a reputable breeder will ask you the same questions you'd be subjected to if you were buying a show-quality dog, because he or she is responsible for what happens to every one of his or her puppies. And you will still want to ask the same questions about breed characteristics, temperament and health.

Don't be put off if the breeder quizzes you, too. This is a good indication that she

It is important that puppies have time to play with their littermates in order to learn how to interact with other dogs.

is a conscientious individual who wants to be sure she is placing the dog she has bred in the best home possible.

A Word About Price

Never let your first question to a breeder be, "How much?" Nothing turns off breeders faster, and after hearing the question that tells them you care more about price than the qualities of the dog, most breeders will show you the door before your second question leaves your lips.

You might spend as much for a purebred dog as you would for a new sofa. But you don't get love from a sofa. Whatever the price you pay, consider it a bargain. Where else can you find a dog whose lineage, breed characteristics, health and temperament are guaranteed?

ADOPTING A PUREBRED DOG

There are several good reasons to adopt a purebred dog. Breeders are committed to maintaining and improving the breeds they love. Each breed has individual characteristics established through centuries of breeding. So when you've decided what characteristics you want in a dog, you know in which breeds you're likely to find them.

Purebred dogs, with health certificates and pedigrees going back several generations, can be expensive. If you can't afford the price but have decided on a purebred, you'll be happy to

Let your child accompany you to the breeder's and play with the puppies you are considering. These German Shorthaired Pointer pups are having a great time with a new friend.

know that purebred dogs or puppies sometimes become available for adoption at minimal cost. For example, a breeder may reclaim a dog when an owner can no longer keep it. Perhaps the owner had difficulty training the dog. Or he had not researched the breed before purchasing, and decided after a few days,

weeks or months that this was not the breed for him. Or the dog did not fit in with other animals in the household. Or he chewed up his favorite shoes. Or has an "accident" on the new carpet. For whatever reason, the pup ends up back at the breeder's through no fault of his own. And that's where you come in.

Reputable breeders consider themselves responsible for puppies they have brought into the world. Although it rarely is convenient for them to find new homes for their dogs after they have sold them, they will sometimes place them in adoptive homes with persons they know will be responsible owners.

If the breeder hasn't yet had the dog neutered or spayed, she will ask you to sign a spay-neuter contract, agreeing that within a certain

How can you pick just one? An adorable bunch of Kuvasz puppies from Karpati Kennels.

number of days you will have this procedure carried out by a veterinarian. All pet dogs should be spayed or neutered. Anyone who is not a serious breeder is seriously irresponsible if he brings puppies into a world already populated by millions of adoptable dogs.

The breeder will also ask you to sign an agreement stating that the dog will be examined by your veterinarian within 48 hours of adoption. No matter where you get your dog, this is an excellent idea.

You'll have the opportunity to talk with the breeder and learn more about the breed and the individual dog. Did unfortunate circumstances lead to the dog's return? Are there learned behaviors you'll have to train him out of?

Adoption through Purebred Rescue

The nationwide scope of

A shelter is a perfect place to get a dog—not only are you gaining a best friend, you are saving a life!

If you do not have the time or inclination to train a puppy, consider adopting an adult. Elizabeth Sussman adopted Max from the Delaware Valley Golden Retriever Rescue.

purebred rescue is truly amazing. Thousands of volunteers in 2000 purebred rescue organizations work tirelessly to place dogs in new homes where they will be loved and cared for.

Advantages in adopting from a purebred rescue organization are that the dog has been screened for health problems, spayed or neutered and inoculated. Each dog is evaluated for temperament, so if a dog is good with children, you'll know right up front.

Rescue workers are in touch with several sources, including breeders, owners, and shelters, and will be in close contact with you during the procedure of adoption and

postadoption adjustment.

Rescue groups encourage breeders to ask for a placement fee, usually about $100, but depending upon the age and health of the dog. For example, one large breed rescue organization suggests these fees: Dogs less than two years old—$200; two to five—$150; five to seven—$100; eight and older—$1.

Often owners or shelters contact rescue workers directly. If a worker knows what breeder the dog is from, she advises the breeder that one of his dogs needs to be reclaimed or re-homed. Either the breeder or rescue person will work with you in introducing the dog to your family. If the breeder is unknown, the dog is placed in a foster home for care and evaluation until a permanent home is found. In foster homes, dogs are kept in clean, safe conditions and are well fed and cared for. They receive regular inoculations and routine veterinarian care. If you get your dog through a

Seasoned citizens deserve to be pampered a little!

purebred rescue organization, you should receive certification that he has been temperament tested, is current on shots, is spayed or neutered and has been tested for heartworm and other parasites.

If you know a veterinarian, ask if he or she knows of any nice, adoptable dogs. Often veterinarians form relationships with purebred rescue organizations and can even direct you to the breed you're looking for. Also, your vet might personally know an adoptable All-American mixed breed sweetie who would make the perfect companion for your kids.

THE ELDERLY DOG

I took into my home a tiny, badly abused, snapping and snarling grey-muzzled dog my daughter had found on the street. Ounce for ounce, he was the meanest dog I've ever met—and the most expensive. He was in pain from a foul-smelling gum infection oozing blood and green pus. His back was roached and his pelvic bones stuck out sharply. I could count his ribs. A heartworm test came back positive. I gently advised my daughter that the best possible thing we could do for the poor, suffering little guy was to let the veterinarian ease him into eternal sleep.

As I said this, the old dog looked deep into my eyes with his cataract-clouded own.

A few thousand dollars later, he was my dog. He appeared to be a purebred, but of course there was no way to be sure. We cured the heartworm, pulled most of the teeth and cleared up the infection, fed him pills in

A senior dog can be a wonderful companion to a gentle, caring child. Eleven-year-old Boxer Ch. Merrilane's April Holiday with friend.

Elderly dogs are quiet, loving and valuable additions to any household.

Take me home! A shelter is a sea of irresistible faces and extraordinary dogs.

peanut butter, and bought him five years he would not otherwise have had. All things considered, they were good years. I know he was grateful, and so was I.

I would not recommend adopting a stray —especially a seriously ill street stray—if you want a companion and teammate for your kids. If you want to be sure what you're getting, invest in a healthy purebred from a reputable kennel. But if you would like to save an elderly and perhaps infirm dog from being euthanized because his owner thinks he is too much trouble or perhaps has died without making arrangements for his pet's care, you will be rewarded a hundredfold for making the old dear's twilight years comfortable and happy.

SHELTERS AND AGENCIES

Your town or county may have a public animal shelter, supported by dog license fees, fines for violations of dog laws, grants and donations.

Not-for-profit adoption agencies often get the "overflow" from municipal shelters. Also, dogs are relinquished directly by owners. These organizations are completely supported by grants, donations and fund-raisers such as community spay-and-neuter days in conjunction with a local veterinary clinic.

The dogs you'll see in the shelter or agency are two-thirds more likely to be All-American than purebred. They don't cost as much. Most shelters charge less than

Reach out and touch somebody's paw—adopt from a shelter!

There is nothing like canine love and affection!

Spaying/neutering is often the best option for your family pet.

$100, and many even include such extras as spaying or neutering, licensing, inoculations, and ID — tags, tattoo or microchip. Sometimes shelters in an area with a high demand for puppies will transport them from an area with an oversupply. If you're looking for a pup, ask when the next group of adoptive youngsters is due.

Before you visit a shelter, be sure all family members agree on what kind of dog you want. When all those eyes look at you from rows of cages, it's hard to resist. You can't take them all home, so keep your mind on why you are there. Walk slowly past all the dogs and take a good look at each one. Then narrow your choice down to the ones you liked best. Walk past the dogs a second time, and a third, fourth, fifth if necessary, narrowing down your choice each time until you've decided on one dog. Don't take a dog home because you feel sorry for him, unless you are sure he is the right dog for you.

Shelters and agencies sometimes offer obedience classes, or they will provide you with a list of "puppy kindergarten" or training classes in your area.

SPAY AND NEUTER

In just six years, one female dog and her offspring can produce 67,000 animals. This statement from The Humane Society of the United States tells you why you should spay or neuter your dog if you are not a serious breeder. It is simply irresponsible not to. Most breeders and shelters provide new owners with a spay/neuter contract, and often pay the veterinarian's bill. In some areas, spayed and neutered dogs are eligible for reduced license fees.

In addition to the obvious benefit—avoiding unwanted litters—are medical and behavioral advantages.

Spayed and neutered dogs are healthier. They are less likely to develop cancer of the reproductive organs. Spaying your female eliminates messy spotting during heat. It also ends unwanted visits by amorous dogs from all over town. You can take a spayed female for walks year-round without fear of being attacked by unleashed males whose owners are less responsible than you.

Spayed females and neutered males are less likely to fight over possessions and territory. Also, male dogs won't roam, break down doors or jump fences in the heat of passion. Neutering eliminates household behavior humans find objectionable, such as "marking" territory on furniture and mounting people's legs.

In both genders, intense sexual frustration is relieved. Your dog becomes a happier, more relaxed, healthier member of the family. What an easy choice.

A girl's best friend. Katie Kennedy and her Aussie pal Chester couldn't be happier together.

If you take good care of your new dog and give him plenty of time and affection, you will have a loving companion for life.

READY, SET, GO!

A NEW NEW DOG OR A NEW OLD DOG?

A puppy was the right choice for the young Banegas children. It can be for your family, too, if you want your kids and their dog to grow up together. Your kids will learn everything there is to know

He'll be less inclined than a teething puppy to snack on the dining room chairs.

Even very old dogs make wonderful pets. If your kids aren't the athletic type and your family prefers quiet time indoors to running around outside with sticks and balls,

table!" that means the dog is fed at doggy dinnertime and not at the table.

Everyone should agree on training procedures; for example, in training the baby puppy to relieve himself outside, someone should be responsible for making sure he goes outdoors at regular two-hour intervals at first—after his nap, after playing, after eating, first thing in the morning and last thing before bed. When he can't be under a watchful eye, usher him into his crate. However, never leave him in the crate for more than two hours. The crate is a training tool and a safe "den" for the pup, not a convenience for his human companions.

This next point might seem like stating the obvious, but if

Even a large dog like Inky the Newfoundland can be trained to be the perfect housepet.

about training and caring for a dog of all ages — starting with housetraining a pup, through all the fun, work and adventure kids and dogs were meant to share, to eventually comforting and caring for an elderly best friend.

Maybe you'll choose an older dog. A mature pooch might already be trained to sit, stay and not relieve himself on the oriental rug.

consider giving a home to a seasoned canine citizen.

YOUR PERFECT DOG?

Before you even think about getting a puppy or older dog, however, be sure every family member is reading from the same page of the owner's manual. All should be in agreement that training will be consistent. If Mom or Dad says, "No begging at the

Crate training is the easiest and fastest way to housebreak your new puppy. This Yorkshire Terrier gets introduced to his new hangout.

you want to avoid all sorts of problems from the get-go, you have to agree on one thing: The pup must know he is a dog, not a person. It is you, not he, who runs the household and gives the orders. This means sleeping in his crate and not on your bed, much less under your covers. You are the boss! Later, once housetraining is accomplished and the pecking order firmly established, you may allow your dog certain privileges, such as joining the family in previously forbidden areas of the house upon which everyone in the family must agree.

Before you bring your dog home, take this checklist to the pet supply store with you, or order from a catalog. Your dog-owning friends who find their mailboxes stuffed with offerings from several pet supply companies will be happy to give you one.

A crate will provide your new puppy will a cozy den to call his own. This Jack Russell Terrier becomes accustomed to his new space.

SHOPPING LIST
- Canine breed reference book
- Canine health care book (not a substitute for sound advice from an expert veterinarian, but an indispensable guide to home health care)
- Crate (a very important item for training and to give pup a snug, secure place all his own)
- Lambswool pad for crate bottom
- Washable dog bed or cushion
- Soft blanket
- Food and water dishes (ceramic is best)
- Assorted chew toys such as Carrot Bone™, Puppybones™, Nylabone® and Gumabone®
- Collar
- Lead
- Toenail trimmers or small cordless grinder
- Brush or grooming pad

Provide your puppy with plenty of safe chew toys, like Nylabones®, to satisfy his chewing needs. This English Bulldog is set for life!

- Doggy toothbrush and toothpaste, such as the 2-Brush™ from Nylabone®
- A first-aid kit which should include:
- Tweezers for removing ticks and thorns
- Scissors
- Nail clippers

The breeder will have started your puppy on the road to good nutrition, so stick to this original diet when you get your puppy home.

Carrots are rich in fiber, carbohydrates, and vitamin A. The Carrot Bone® by Nylabone® is a durable chew containing no plastics or artificial ingredients and it can be served as-is, in a bone-hard form, or microwaved into a biscuity consistency.

- Roll of gauze
- Bandages
- Two-inch roll of adhesive
- Square gauze
- Antiseptic cream
- Cotton balls
- Small plastic jar for stool or urine sample
- Ear and eye drops.

Also, stock up on food. A puppy will have been weaned by the time he's eight weeks old, so don't bother with milk. He doesn't need it any more, and it will only give him gas and diarrhea. Continue giving him the same food on which his breeder weaned him.

Changing homes is stressful no matter what his age, so keep changes, including diet, to a minimum for the first week or two. Pet food companies offer a variety of foods specially formulated for puppies. If you decide to change food after consulting with your vet, do so gradually, mixing the old brand with the new brand.

If your dog is older, there's a food formulated for his time in life. Check with other dog owners and your vet. Your dog also will be happy to provide input. If he turns up his delicate nose at kibble, mix in a little soft dog food for flavor. To add an irresistible bouquet that will tempt even the most jaded canine palate, heat your culinary achievement in the microwave at medium for 30 seconds.

Have a good supply of chew toys ready for the big day. Dogs of all ages love to chew; better a Galileo™ or Gumaball™ than your damask-upholstered tub chair. Gnawing on a Roar-Hide™ chew not only satisfies your dog's irresistible urge to chew, but also helps keep his teeth clean and tartar-free. Oral disease is one of the most frequently diagnosed diseases in dogs of all ages. According to a recent study by the University of Minnesota, 80 percent of dogs show signs of gum disease by the time they're three years old. Manifestations include tartar buildup, inflamed gums and loss of teeth. And the breath!

Other good chews are edible Carrot Bones™, Gumabone® Plaque Attacker™ and Hercules™. Stuff a sterilized marrow bone with cheese spread or peanut butter and store it in the freezer. That's a hard-to-beat treat after a game of catch on a hot day.

PUPPY-PROOF YOUR HOUSE

You already know this drill. Remember when your human baby started to crawl, walk and explore and you had to

POPpups® are 100% edible and enhanced with dog-friendly ingredients like liver, cheese, spinach, chicken, carrots, or potatoes. They contain no salt, sugar, alcohol, plastic, or preservatives. You can even microwave a POPpup® to turn it into a huge crackly treat.

move everything breakable out of reach and put under lock and key all harmful substances? This time it will be easier because you have a kid to help you do it. Never for one second doubt the ability of a puppy to climb where it shouldn't climb, pry cabinet doors open with a paw, nudge partly-closed doors open with a nose, steal socks, shred slippers, decimate draperies, and invent mischief you haven't yet imagined.

Fat Albert, aka Big Al, a black-and-white English Springer Spaniel from West Chicago, Illinois, even learned to open the refrigerator before his first birthday. After doing so, he ate five steaks and several hot dogs.

A liver-and-white Springer, Louisa, aka Mooshums of Huntington, New York, celebrated Easter while her family was at church by scootching a bed across the floor to a dresser upon which

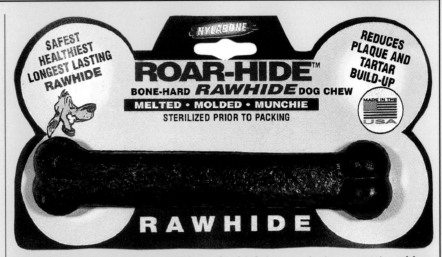

Roar-Hide® is completely edible and is high in protein (over 86%) and low in fat (less than one-third of 1%). Unlike common rawhide, it is safer, less messy, and more fun for your dog.

sat four baskets filled to the brim with jelly beans, coconut cream eggs, marshmallow chicks, dyed hardboiled eggs, mixed nuts and carob bunnies. She polished off everything except the carob bunnies. When her family arrived home, she greeted them by regurgitating at their feet her entire Easter feast.

Although disgusting by human standards, these gustatory escapades did no lasting harm. Unfortunately,

The 2-Brush® by Nylabone® is made with two toothbrushes to clean both sides of your dog's teeth at the same time. Each brush contains a reservoir designed to apply the toothpaste, which is specially formulated for dogs, directly into the toothbrush.

All puppies have an inherent desire to chew. Blitzen the Min Pin attacks his favorite toy.

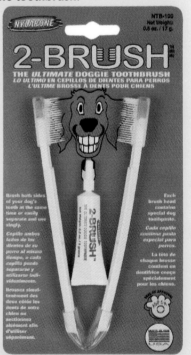

other, more dangerous, substances are attractive to dogs. If the carob bunnies, inspired no doubt by a parental impulse toward healthy fare, had been chocolate, Mooshems undoubtedly would have wolfed them down and become seriously ill. Chocolate can even be lethal to dogs.

Automobile antifreeze fluid is another substance that smells good, tastes good, and is fatal. Several household and garden plants and bulbs cause sickness and death.

All the world is new to a puppy, and he wants to explore everything. It's up to

Certain plants and flowers are poisonous to your dogs. Always closely supervise your dog when outside.

harmful plants and substances, loose garbage can lids, and anything you don't want eaten.

Some foods, like chocolate, can be dangerous, even lethal, to dogs. Make sure to keep "people food" out of your dogs reach.

A gate can be useful in keeping your dog confined to safe areas of your house. These Golden Retriever adult and puppy try to get a peek at what's going on.

you to protect him from harm, and your family from heartbreak.

Get rid of or keep behind securely closed doors well out of reach anything that can harm your precious new family member.

The same rules apply to mature and elderly dogs as well as puppies. Even though older dogs are somewhat more blasé than puppies about putting everything in sight into their mouths, err on the side of caution and don't put temptation in their paths. Use common sense in conducting a safety sweep of your house and yard, with a sharp eye out for gaps in the fence,

HOUSEHOLD PRODUCTS

These products are dangerous to your dog:

- Prescription and over-the-counter medications
- Antifreeze, gasoline, oil and other car and mechanical fluids
- Rodent poison
- Slug or snail poison
- Bleach and other household chemicals
- Matches and matchbooks
- Mothballs
- Skin, nail and hair products
- Deodorants and fragrances
- Detergents and cleaning fluid
- Insecticides and tick repellants
- Herbicides
- Lighter fluid
- Lantern oil
- Paint
- Alcohol
- Turpentine

Be sure to pick a dog food that is nutritious and is adequate for your dog's stage of life.

Digging can be a sign that your dog is bored. Make sure your dog has plenty of toys and activities to keep him out of mischief.

jerusalem cherry, jimson weed, juniper, larkspur, laurel, lily of the valley, mistletoe, morning glory, needlepoint ivy, oleander, oxallis, philodendrom, podocarpus, poison ivy, poison sumac, poison hemlock, poison oak, pokeberry, potato plant, pothos, pyracantha, rhododendron, rhubarb, skunk cabbage, snow on the mountain, spathe flower, string of pearls, tomato leaves, violet seeds, wild carrots, wild cucumber, wild parsnip, wild peas and yew tree.

Many other plants, though less poisonous, can cause adverse reactions in sensitive animals. You should be able to obtain a complete list and illustrations for identification from your veterinarian, local garden club, or library.

POISONOUS PLANTS

These plants contain various poisons that cause symptoms ranging from skin rashes to kidney damage in humans and animals: amaryllis, azalea, begonia, bird of paradise, black nightshade berry, butterfly weed, calla lily, calamondin orange tree, carnation, castor bean, christmas cherry, cyclamen, daffodil flower and bulb, daisy, daphne, deadly nightshade, devils ivy, diffenbachia, dumbcane, english holly, english ivy, elderberry, elephant ears, eucalyptus, eyebane, firecracker, foxglove, geranium, golden chain, holly berry, horse chestnut, hyacinth, hydrangea blossom, iris, jack- in- the-pulpit, jequirity bean,

With all the chaos, lights, and small ornaments, the holidays can be an especially dangerous time to bring home a small puppy.

The care that you give to your dog will be evident in his shiny coat, bright eyes and overall healthy appearance.

TEAMMATES: A WORLD OF FUN, FRIENDS AND FUZZY FACES

When Hector and Annie began their search for the perfect dog, their first consideration was: "How will a dog fit into the way our family lives?" They knew they wanted a canine companion to make their family complete, so they started looking for a pet everyone could enjoy. They liked outdoor activity, so the dog couldn't be a stay-at-home couch potato. They enjoyed visiting with friends of all ages, so the dog must possess a friendly nature and be relatively easy to train. Hector and Annie enjoy a daily run, so their ideal dog would, too.

If your child shows interest in participating in an informal

Play and exercise benefit not only your dog, but your kids as well. This Australian Shepherd retrieves his Gumabone® Frisbee®.

The amount of activity your child enjoys should be a consideration when selecting a dog. A breed like the energetic Border Collie thrives with plenty of exercise.

or organized activity with the dog, this consideration will guide your selection. Dogs love to play. They need regular exercise. So do kids. Hours of play-exercise every day benefit humans, dog and furniture. A well-exercised dog is a dog that won't put his energy into chewing on your Chippendale.

The special bond between your kids and their canine companion can be strengthened by spur-of-the-moment activities such as swimming, jogging, hiking, or fast-paced backyard games such as regulation Frisbee™, Gumabone® Frisbee™, agility, or flyball.

You can take these activities one step farther and

Agility is just one of the many organized events that your dog and child can do together. This English Springer Spaniel competes in the agility tire jump.

Your dog will enjoy playing with his Gumabone® Frisbee®—he is not only exercising his jaw when he chews, but the molded bone on top makes it easy to pick up.

on the grounds of the Washington Monument in Washington, D.C. Leading up to the grand championship are 7 regional competitions and 126 local events at which novices are welcome. To get started, send a SASE to Skyhoundz, 4060-D Peachtree Road, Ste. 326 G, Atlanta, GA 30319 for schedules and instructions.

Gumabone® Frisbee™ gives your dog an energy-intensive two-fer—a great workout and a satisfying chew afterwards. When your dog stops playing to gnaw on his Gumabone® Frisbee™, he's exercising his jaw muscles. The chewing also helps keep his teeth free of tartar, the number-one cause of gum disease that can lead to other serious canine diseases.

Some breeds have inherent talents and will excel in certain events. The Newfoundland is an excellent swimmer and can be trained for swimming trials or as a water rescue dog.

enter competitive events. Before taking your dog on the playing field, however, be sure your veterinarian gives him a complete physical and all his shots.

FRISBEE™

Frisbee™ dogs are a familiar sight in parks, at beaches and at special events. Not every dog can be an Ashley Whippet or a Soaring Sam, but some dogs seem to have a knack for defying the law of gravity as they leap to catch the flying disc.

My English Springer Spaniel Kipper loved Frisbee®. Every evening when my husband came in the door, she'd trot up to him with her Frisbee™ in her mouth. He'd throw high, low, far, wide and she'd catch every one until she flopped down in the grass, tongue lolling out the side of her grinning mouth.

At the annual Alpo Canine Frisbee™ Championships, top dogs soar for the flying discs

The special bond that forms between your child and your dog while practicing obedience is a strong one. Abby Banegas teaches Jimmy to sit.

FLYBALL

To play flyball, all you need is a specially designed box with a lever on it and a bucket full of balls in one of two sizes —small for tiny Toy-breed dynamos and regular for all other sizes. Fill the box with balls and watch the fun. Your dog runs up to the box and bats the lever, which catapults a ball through the air. Your dog runs, jumps and catches the ball on the fly. Another great way for booth your dog and your kid to work off excess energy!

In some flyball competitions, the dogs snag the ball and tear around a track. The first dog to finish wins! In formal competition, dogs snag and race in relays.

For information on Flyball competition, write the North American Flyball Association, P.O. Box 8, Mt. Hope, ONT, Canada, LOR IWO.

Meadow's Fantasia, CD, OA, a Bearded Collie owned by Antoinette Krafcheck, tries her hand at the agility teeter totter.

AGILITY

Agility is a wonderful way for your kid and dog to get fit and stay fit. This sport, which originated in England, has taken American dogdom by storm. In 1985, the United States Dog Agility Association (USDAA) was formed for all dogs. In 1994, the AKC launched an Agility division. In October, a United States

Agility is an action-packed sport that is thrilling for both participants and spectators alike.

An Airedale Terrier conquers the bar jump.

AKC Team competes in the World Agility Championship.

Agility organizations give demonstrations at most major dog and horse shows. After the demo, spectators and their dogs line up to try it out. You and your dog are a team, covering the obstacle course together. Everyone is excited. The dogs are eager to get onto the course, and their human companions clap and congratulate one another. It's great fun to run beside your dog, shouting encouragement as he goes over the A-frame, through the weave poles, across the dog walk and through the tire jump! You'll be able to tell the very first time if your dog has an aptitude for agility.

If there's an agility club in your area, your kid and dog can make agility practice an enjoyable weekend outing, and perhaps train for bigger and better things. More and more clubs are getting into agility. Your club can build the equipment or send away for it. If there's no organization nearby, you can set up an agility course in the backyard. Plans for jumps, tunnels, ramps, a-frames and other obstacles are available from the major organizations and from companies that advertise in dog publications. You can purchase them ready-made, but it's a lot less expensive to build them. A good weekend project for the family. Mom? Dad?

Frisbee™, flyball and agility are great backyard games. It's also fun to make these informal events the centerpiece of a birthday party—your kid's or your dog's—with all the neighborhood dogs in attendance.

If your dog is a keen athlete and your child has a genuine interest in dog-related activities and careers, the sky's the limit. Dog clubs, local and national organizations and pet food companies sponsor a wide array of activities and competitions your children and dog can enjoy together as teammates. There's something for everydog!

JUNIOR SHOWMANSHIP

The American Kennel Club's Junior Showmanship program opens a whole new world of fun, friends, travel, excitement and education to kids who love dogs and have a commitment to their welfare. The program gives kids an opportunity to learn about dogs, their care, and their presentation at shows. It's a great way to meet other kids who are interested in dogs

and the standard of the breed. They'll learn how to present their dogs in the ring and themselves in any social or business situation. It's great preparation for a successful life.

Judging criteria for the Novice class and the more advanced Open class are:
- Proper breed presentation
- Skill in presenting the individual's dog
- Knowledge of ring procedures
- Appearance and conduct.

Winners in the classes

Junior handling is a wonderful way for a young person to build confidence and start a successful career in showing.

Exchange Program, a two-week summer event in the U.S. and England, is supported partially by all-breed clubs. The Hockamock

A junior handler is judged solely on his ability to handle his dog, not on the dog's conformation.

Junior Showmanship teaches good sportsmanship, correct dog handling and canine care.

and knowledgeable adults who can help your kids get started in the sport of purebred dogs.

The Junior Showmanship program emphasizes good sportsmanship and self-confidence, along with a thorough knowledge of dogs, the junior's chosen breed and the rules and etiquette of the show ring. Your kids will learn basic grooming, nutrition, emergency medical care, anatomy, business skills, transportation, social skills,

compete for the title of Best Junior Handler.

Many dog clubs offer weekly handling classes where kids can learn the basics. Also, some clubs have instituted formal programs to match knowledgable adults with kids who show they're eager to learn about the sport. Also, professional handlers and owner-handlers kids meet at shows and clubs can tell them about programs and competitions.

The Junior Handlers

The development of self-confidence and social skills are just some of the advantages to participating in Junior Showmanship.

A dog that passes his Canine Good Citizenship test will be a wonderful and tolerant companion to any child. This Rottweiler watches over his charges.

In order to become a Canine Good Citizen, your dog must be able to get along with people, including children. This American Water Spaniel seems to have passed the test!

Rules and Regulations for Junior Showmanship.

CANINE GOOD CITIZEN

At dog events across the country, kids and their dogs are lining up to take the Canine Good Citizenship test. It's fun for you and your kids to prepare your pooch for CGC certification. You'll teach him to come, sit, down, heel, stay and behave well in any situation. You and your dog will learn to trust each other.

The "Come" command is the most important your dog will ever learn. When he hears it, he'll stop whatever he is doing—jumping on a guest, getting too rowdy with small children or other dogs, planning an escape from the yard—and run to you. This basic command may even save your dog's life if he is heading for a busy street or into any other kind of danger. For tips on teaching "Come," see the Obedience section.

(Mass.) Kennel Club, Connecticut's Elm City Kennel Club and Providence County (R.I.) Kennel Club hold matches and meet-the-judges luncheons during the program. American participants must complete a questionnaire and be able to host a British junior for the U.S. half of the program. Contact coordinator Lynn D. Cherico at 508-226-0311.

The Dog Writers' Educational Trust provides college scholarships for young

This Labrador retriever has decided its time to play ball!

people interested in the world of dogs or who have participated in Junior Showmanship classes in the United States or Canada. The scholarships are available in any field of study, with designated grants for students of mass communications and journalism. More than 200 grants totaling in excess of $170,000 have been awarded since 1975. Application deadline each year is August 1. Contact Mary Ellen Tarman, Executive Secretary, Dog Writers' Educational Trust, P.O. Box E, Hummelstown, PA 17036-0199.

Most breed clubs offer awards to outstanding junior showing the breed at their national specialties.

For information about the Junior Showmanship program, write the AKC, 5580 Centerview Drive, Raleigh, NC 27606, and ask for the brochures *Getting Started in Junior Showmanship* and

The Canine Good Citizen Test has ten steps. A trained evaluator will judge your dog on:

1. Accepting a Friendly Stranger—This test shows that your dog will allow a stranger to approach and talk to you or your kids in an average, everyday manner. Your dog will sit quietly and not lunge or jump in greeting. Your kids can practice by stopping to talk to neighbors when they walk the dog.

2. Sitting Politely for Petting —Your dog shows that he can accept attention without getting frightened, excited or resentful. Start training him by putting him in the sit position while family members pet him. When he can do this, ask friends and other people to pet him, so he will become accustomed to this attention without becoming flustered.

3. Appearance and Grooming—Your child must groom the dog for his CGC debut. Your pooch's appearance should tell the examinator that he is well cared for. Also, during the test, the dog must allow the evaluator to brush him and examine his ears and front feet. You can prepare your dog for this by making grooming a pleasant event. Talk to him gently while examining ears and feet. Give a treat after brushing.

4. Walking on a Loose Lead—Your child and dog should walk well together. The evaluator will ask them to turn left, turn right and about turn, with at least one stop in between and another at the end. Your dog does not have to heel, and can be on on your child's left or right side.
   When lead training your dog, have your child hold the end of the lead in his or her right hand, and with the left hand hold the lead so that he or she can control the dog's movements at all times.

5. Walking through a Crowd—Your dog must show that he can move through a crowd without

A well-groomed appearance is an important part of the Canine Good Citizen Test.

getting excited or fearful. Kids should practice by walking the dog on busy sidewalks or through playgrounds. Gradually introduce him to situations where there are more and more people. Of course, you don't want to expose a puppy to other dogs and crowds of people until he has had all his inoculations to protect against disease.

6. Sit, Down and Stay on Command—This test shows how well your dog is trained. The lead is replaced by a 20-foot rope supplied by the evaluator. When your child gives the commands, the dog must stay in place until the evaluator gives the release command. Practice at home by gently guiding the dog into position and staying nearby when he is in the stay. Gradually add distractions and move farther and farther away until the dog holds the stay for two to three minutes.
   Kids and dogs attend obedience classes to learn the basic commands. Tips for training are in the obedience section.

7. Coming When Called—This is your dog's chance to show how well he has learned his most important lesson. The dog is on the 20-foot line that was used in Step 6. Your child will walk 10 feet from the dog, turn to face the dog and call him. If the dog tries to follow the owner, the evaluator may distract the dog by petting until the owner is

10 feet away. When the dog comes, your child attaches his own lead. "Come" is the first lesson you and your kids teach your dog, so this will be the easiest part of the CGC test for you. Practice it over and over again, every day.

8. Reaction to Another Dog—This test shows that your dog can remain calm near another dog. As the evaluator watches, your child and another owner will walk with their dogs toward each other. They meet, shake hands, and say a few words, then continue on their way for about five yards. Your child's dog should not go to the other dog or the other dog's owner.
   To practice for this part of the test, put your dog in a Stay whenever you're out walking and another dog approaches. Keep your dog in the Stay until the other dog passes.
   Encourage your kids to practice this with their

A well-mannered dog will be welcomed in any home.

friends who have dogs.

9. Reaction to Distractions—This shows that your dog can remain calm and confident around the normal noises and activities outside your home. The evaluator will shout or make another loud noise. He'll also flap a coat in front of your dog or create some other sight distraction. The dog should not cringe, try to run away, bark or show aggression.

You dog should be able to meet strange people or animals without becoming fearful or aggressive. Hunter, a Siberian Husky, says hello to some horses.

Socialize your dog with all kinds of people. This St. Bernard gets along with the whole family.

From the time your dog is a pup, walk him where there are traffic noises and other loud sounds so he'll get used to hearing them without becoming upset. At home, drop a book at a distance from the dog. Gradually bring the distraction closer. If your dog shows fear, move back and bring it closer more slowly. Outside, have a friend jog past your dog so he'll get used to seeing a person or another animal moving without wanting to give chase. Praise him when he gets it right.

10. Supervised Separation—The last step in the CGC test demonstrates that your dog can be left with another person while you go out of sight. You give the lead to the evaluator and walk away out of sight. Your dog doesn't

have to stand still, but he should not bark, howl, pace back and forth, or show nervousness or fear.

Never tie your dog and leave him while you go on an errand. Never allow a stranger to hold him except in the most dire emergency. But you should be able to leave him for a few minutes with someone he has never seen before, but whom you know.

At home, put your dog in the stay position and leave the room for a few seconds, gradually leaving him for longer periods of time. Say something like, "I'll be right back," so he knows he doesn't

Good Citizen Test and training tips, contact the American Kennel Club, CGC Department, 5580 Centerview Drive, Raleigh, NC 27606, or call 919-233-9767.

OBEDIENCE

Before your kid and dog try any of these challenging, fun-filled activities, it's absolutely essential for them to learn the basic obedience commands. A well-mannered dog that works well with its owner is welcome in competitive events with other dogs.

Obedience classes are valuable not only to teach your dog the basics, but also

An obedience class will not only teach your dog basic commands, it will help socialize him in a safe, friendly environment.

have to stay in position, but knows he should wait for you without fussing.

Dog clubs, obedience schools, community colleges, scouts, 4-H and other organizations may administer a CGC test. For a copy of the complete 10-step Canine

to socialize him properly in a safe, friendly environment. To find a good obedience school or instructor in your area, check with owners and handlers at dog shows.

It's your kid's job to work with the dog every day, to make sure the lessons are learned and reinforced. As a parent, it's your job to encourage your kid to train himself or herself, too, to be consistent, patient, upbeat and in command at all times.

There's a time for play and a time for work. Your dog will respond best if your kid works with him at the same times every day, for no more than 10 minutes at a time. Always end the training session with lots of praise, a romp and a treat—preferably one that satisfies your dog's urge to chew—such as Nylabone®, Puppybones® or Roar-Hide®, made from rawhide that is ground, melted, sterilized and re-formed into a solid bone-hard chew that will not break

Training classes are a great place for your dog to interact with other dogs. This Labrador and Westie pup give each other the once-over.

With basic obedience training, who knows how far you can go? Parker, owned by Robert Handshuh, is the first Afghan Hound to receive an AKC agility title.

down into strings that can threaten your dog's health.

Also, check your local book store and library for books and videos on obedience training. There's one for every size dog and every training method.

The first basic commands taught at doggy school are: Come, Sit, Down, Stay.

Come

After you've acclimated your pup to his collar and leash, say his name and then "Come," in a no-nonsense but pleasant

voice, giving a gentle tug on the leash. When he comes to you, say "Good Come!" in a happy voice. Repeat several times.

The next day, put your dog on a longer lead and let him move farther away from you before giving the command. By the end of a week, allow him to roam at the end of a 30-foot rope before you call his name and "Come!" and reel him in to a great deal of praise and a treat. Do this over and over again. After a few days, do it on and off the rope, of course in your fenced-in yard or other enclosed area. Then do it completely off the rope. When baby lapses—and he will—it's back on the rope for a few sessions before doing it freel-style again. Practice the "Come!" command every day of your dog's life.

Sit

When teaching this

command, don't apply pressure to your dog's back or you might hurt her. Holding a treat above her head, move it back, so as she looks at it, her muzzle will rise and her hindquarters will sink. She should naturally back into a sitting position. If she backs up instead of sitting, gently move your hand from her neck down her back to urge her into a sit. When she accomplishes this, say, "Good sit! Gooood sit!" Do this several times. Later that day, so it some more. Repeat every day, alternating with "Come!"

Down

This can be a more difficult command, since it might bring up issues of dominance. Start teaching the Down yourself before turning instruction over to your kid. When your kid teaches the Down, he must be gentle but always firm and in command.

Providing your dog with basic training shows him you care about his well being and his future as a family member. This Wirehaired Pointing Griffon puppy shows his thanks!

This German Shepherd puppy fostered by Chris Chambers is in training to become a Future Leader Dog.

Bring the treat down to the floor, so that the dog follows it with his head, while you gently urge him down with your other hand. When he is completely down, give him the treat and praise him. Repeat, repeat, repeat. On the next session, do Come and Sit. Then do Come and Down.

Stay

With your dog in the Sit or Down, hold your hand, palm forward, in front of her face and say, "Stay!" Then back away from her. If she stays for one second before following her, praise her! Next time, try for two seconds, and so on. Gradually, work up to five minutes. If you work at the

China knows her Australian Shepherd is well trained and will stay by her side while they enjoy a game of fetch.

in your area. Matches, held by all-breed or specialty (single-breed) clubs, or by organizations that include All-American mutts as well as purebred dogs, are low-pressure proving grounds. They give dogs and owners opportunities to practice for the big time or simply enjoy a day of socializing and seeing how their pooches stack up against the competition. Spayed or neutered dogs may compete in all three levels of obedience—novice, open and Utility. These lead to the titles Companion Dog (CD), Companion Dog Excellent (CDX) and Utility Dog (UD) respectively.

In novice obedience, your dog learns six exercises: heel on lead, stand for examination, heel free, recall, long sit and long down. In open work, she does seven exercises: heel free, drop (down) on recall, retrieve on flat, retrieve over the high jump, broad jump, long sit and long down. Utility work consists of five exercises: a signal exercise,

There is no limit to what your dog can do with the right training—even if it is just splashing in the pool! These two Australian Cattle Dogs join their friends for a dip.

Stay consistently, you should be able to leave the room for a few minutes and return to find her still in the Stay. This takes time and patience.

Your dog will also learn to heel, staying close by your left side. You and your kid can prepare her for obedience heeling lessons by training her to walk on lead without pulling or lunging.

Discuss with a knowledgable trainer what kind of collar and lead is best for your dog.

While you are practicing these basic exercises, try to fit in some other activities for variety, such as tracking, jumping and retrieving.

If your kid and dog take to obedience like a frisky pup to a Chick-n-Cheez Chooz™, encourage them to venture forth and enter a fun match

Sharlow's Irish Sundancer, CD, a Golden Retriever owned by Neva Sharlow, participates in a "Prevent A Bite" program.

two scent-discrimination tests, directed retrieve, directed jumping and group examination.

COMMUNITY SERVICE

In addition to competing in the sport of dogs, your kid and dog can perform a community service. Local kennel clubs and obedience schools offer therapy dog training courses where your dog can learn the proper behavior for visiting hospitals, nursing homes and home health care patients. What a difference your dog can make in the lives of people who don't have their own dogs to bring them comfort and happiness!

When I took my elderly adopted Min Pin, Brutus, on a weekly visit to a local nursing home, residents who were depressed and unresponsive most of the time eagerly approached us. Brutus, who was in his late teens and often cranky, rose to the occasion and was on his best behavior. I held him as the residents

With the help of Sharlow's Irish Sundancer, these children are learning dog safety.

touched and petted him. They all had stories to tell about former pets. How they missed their animal companions! Sometimes Brutus would change the script and scamper about the lounge, causing laughter and merriment on every side. I know my little dog made a difference in the nursing home residents' lives. Your Therapy Team can do a good thing, too.

Another way in which your kid can contribute to the community is by taking his well-trained dog to school, either as part of an organized effort or as an individual, with the approval of his teacher and administration.

Abby took Jimmy the Beagle to school. She told her class about the breed and dogs in general, and showed them how Jimmy had learned to sit and stay. She told her classmates how to act with a dog, and they took turns talking to Jimmy and petting him. It was a great learning experience for the class and a welcome break for kids and teacher. Jimmy enjoyed the attention. Warning—do this only if your child's teacher determines that others in the class will not be disruptive!

Therapy dogs can provide a world of joy and comfort to those in nursing homes or hospitals. This Westie makes a new friend.

SUGGESTED READING

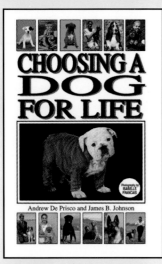

TS-257
Choosing A Dog for Life
Andrew DePrisco and James
B. Johnson
384 pages, over 700 full-color
photos.

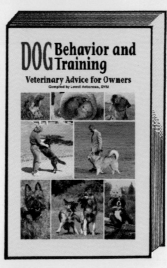

TS-252
Dog Behavior and Training
Dr. Lowell Ackerman, DVM
292 pages, over 200 full-color
photos.

TS-258
**Training Your Dog for Sports
and Other Activities**
Charlotte Schwartz
160 pages, over 200 full-color
photos.

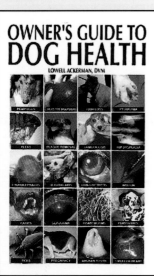

TS-214
Owner's Guide to Dog Health
Dr. Lowell Ackerman, DVM
423 pages, over 300 full-color
photos.

TS-205
Successful Dog Training
Michael Kamer, O.S.B.
160 pages, over 130 full-color
photos.

TS-249
Skin and Coat Care for Your Dog
Dr. Lowell Ackerman, DVM
224 pages, over 190 full-color
photos.